An Introduction to Interdisciplinary Research

An Introduction to Interdisciplinary Research

Theory and Practice

Edited by

Steph Menken

Machiel Keestra

Authors

Lucas Rutting

Ger Post

Machiel Keestra

Mieke de Roo

Sylvia Blad

Linda de Greef

Amsterdam University Press

Volume 2 of the Series Perspectives on Interdisciplinarity

Cover design and lay-out: Matterhorn Amsterdam

Amsterdam University Press English-language titles are distributed in the US and Canada by the University of Chicago Press.

ISBN   978 94 6298 184 3
e-ISBN   978 90 4853 161 5
NUR   100

Contents

Acknowledgements

This handbook is based on almost 20 years of experience with interdisciplinary studies of the authors, editors and others involved in writing this book. The materials and practices of the University of Amsterdam's (UvA) Institute for Interdisciplinary Studies (IIS) contributed significantly to the approach that we have adopted.
We are also grateful to all the people who read drafts and provided useful feedback and critical commentary. In alphabetical order, they are:

- Prof. dr. F.A. Bais
  Institute for Theoretical Physics (ITFA), Faculty of Science, UvA
  External faculty member of the Santa Fe Institute
- Prof. dr. K. van Dam
  Emeritus Professor at the UvA and founder of the IIS
- Prof. dr. J.A.E.F. van Dongen
  ITFA and IIS, Faculty of Science, UvA
  Institute for History and Foundations of Science, Utrecht University
- Dr. R. van der Lecq
  Department of Philosophy and Religious Studies, Utrecht University
- Prof. dr. W.H. Newell
  Emeritus Professor of Interdisciplinary Studies, Miami University, USA
  Executive Director and Past President of the Association for Interdisciplinary Studies
- Dr. T.J. Schuitmaker
  Athena Institute, Faculty of Earth and Life Sciences, VU University Amsterdam
- Prof. dr. R. Szostak
  Full Professor, Economics Department, University of Alberta, Canada
  Past President of the Association for Interdisciplinary Studies
- Dr. J.C. Tromp
  IIS, Faculty of Science, UvA
- Ms L.U. Wenting, MSc
  Director IIS, Faculty of Science, UvA

We also greatly appreciate the support and feedback of the program directors, lecturers and students of various bachelor and master programs, in particular:

- Mr J. ter Schegget, MSc – Bachelor Bèta-gamma
- Prof. dr. W. Bouten – Bachelor Future Planet Studies
- Mr H.B. de Vries, MSc – Bachelor Interdisciplinary Social Sciences
- Ms R. van Wieringen, MSc – Bachelor Interdisciplinary Social Sciences
- Ms M.A. van Eenbergen, MSc – Bachelor Interdisciplinary Social Sciences
- Dr. F. Nack – Master Information Studies
- Ms S.M. van Beekum, MSc – Master Brain and Cognitive Sciences
- Mr J.J. Klingen, BSc – student Future Planet Studies
- Mr B. Cornelissen – student Bèta-gamma

Preface

An Introduction to Interdisciplinary Research is a handbook on interdisciplinarity and its background, and a manual on conducting interdisciplinary research for undergraduates and beyond. Although several books have been written about interdisciplinary research, providing rich theoretical descriptions of and hands-on approaches to the topic, this handbook is a more condensed resource focusing on students in the social and natural sciences. The most relevant comparison can be drawn with Allen Repko's seminal *Interdisciplinary Research: Process and Theory*, 2nd ed. (2012). Repko's book served as an important source of inspiration and information for us. Having used Repko's book for several years in our interdisciplinary research seminars, we felt the need for another book that would differ in several respects from Repko's valuable book. As a result, our book mainly focuses on European students, whereas Repko's book seems to be primarily addressing undergraduate students from institutions in the US and Canada. This is why our book primarily contains examples of research carried out in Europe. Furthermore, we focus on students with majors in the social and natural sciences and less on those who major in the humanities or liberal arts and sciences. We have also included a thorough description of complexity, which we and others consider to be a main driving force behind interdisciplinarity. However, the most significant difference to Repko's manual concerns size. We explicitly aimed to produce a more condensed book that is practical, to the point, and clear.

The book is divided into three parts. The first part – *The Handbook* – gives a brief overview of interdisciplinarity and provides fundamental information about the origins of interdisciplinary research, what it entails, when it can be applied, and why it should be applied. The second part of the book – *The Manual* – focuses on the step-by-step process and sets out instructions on how to undertake interdisciplinary research. The third part contains a model example of an interdisciplinary project and the career stories of some interdisciplinary scholars.
Many questions surround interdisciplinary research. How does it differ from disciplinary research? What does it demand from the interdisciplinary researcher? What potential does it have that disciplinary research does not offer? It is important to note that interdisciplinary research builds on disciplinary research. When dealing with complex problems, a merely disciplinary approach will not suffice. Such problems necessitate an interdisciplinary approach when scientifically and socially robust answers are sought.

The interdisciplinary research process is not an easy journey. In fact, it is a challenge for undergraduate students and experienced senior researchers alike. The aim of this book is to make the process more accessible. We provide many examples of interdisciplinary research projects, obstacles that researchers encounter during their academic journey, and the solutions they came up with. Moreover, we interviewed researchers who are experienced in applying an interdisciplinary approach, and we share their expert insights.

It would have been impossible to write this book without the contributions of the experts, lecturers, students and other individuals affiliated with the IIS at the UvA. We hope that you enjoy it, that you will learn a lot while reading it, and that you put the insights obtained into practice. We also welcome your feedback, so if you come across mistakes, or have suggestions to improve it, please get in touch with us via L.degreef@uva.nl.

Chapter guides

The first part of the handbook begins with a short introduction to the main topic of the book (chapter 1). Next we give an explanation of what science actually is; in other words, we will dive into the philosophy of science (chapter 2), after which we define what an academic discipline is, and provide a description of the historical development of the current disciplinary structure of the academic system (chapter 3). We then describe how this division into disciplines evolved (also in chapter 3), and thereafter we move on to define multidisciplinarity, transdisciplinarity, and interdisciplinarity (chapter 4). This is followed by an overview of the most relevant drivers of interdisciplinary research, which, in our view, share one characteristic: complexity (chapter 5). Part 1 concludes with a feature that is unique to interdisciplinary research: the integration of disciplinary insights at different levels (chapter 6). This is where interdisciplinary research differs from multidisciplinary research.

After reading part 1, you should have acquired enough knowledge to start your own interdisciplinary research project. Part 2 will guide you through this process by means of a model for interdisciplinary research introduced in chapter 7. It points out where monodisciplinary and interdisciplinary research approaches differ, and gives a step-by-step explanation of the process from the problem definition (chapter 8), the formulation of the research question (chapter 9), and data collection and analysis (chapter 10) to the discussion and conclusions (chapter 11).

Then, in part 3 (chapter 12), we start with an example of an interdisciplinary research project following the steps of our model, introduced in part 2. Furthermore, we share the stories about the careers of four interdisciplinary scholars in chapter 13.

Part 1
The Handbook
'The What'

1 Introduction

Half a century ago, philosopher of science Karl Popper (1963) famously observed: "We are not students of some subject matter, but students of problems. And problems may cut right across the boundaries of any subject matter or discipline." This statement has become increasingly relevant. Today, many of the phenomena and problems that we are trying to understand and solve indeed 'cut across' the traditional boundaries of academic disciplines. Modern technological developments and globalization add to the complexity of problems and, in response, we are becoming increasingly aware that an integrated approach is necessary. Healthcare, climate change, food security, energy, financial markets, and quality of life are but a few examples of subjects that drive scientists to 'cross borders' and engage with experts from multiple fields to find solutions. In short, complex questions and problems necessitate an interdisciplinary approach to research.

Most real-life problems are multifaceted, in that they have multiple types of causes and determining factors. These different types of causes and determining factors often have to be addressed in different ways with different disciplinary methods. We know from research, for example, that alcohol intake is involved in over half of the violent acts that take place in the public domain. However, the relationship between the intake of alcohol and aggressive behavior is much more complex, and different disciplines have different perspectives on this relationship, as you can see in figure 1. Each discipline's focus is on another factor (in this case either nurture- of nature-related) at a different level of analysis, using different theoretical frameworks, and different methodologies.

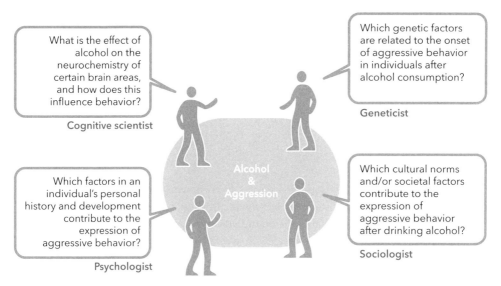

Figure 1 Different perspectives on the relationship between alcohol intake and aggression

Another example of a multifaceted problem is the financial crisis. Over the past five years, academics from different disciplines have tried to explain what caused the global economic recession. These disciplinary explanations, however, only shed light on part of the problem. When combined, they may offer a more comprehensive explanation, as you can see below in figure 2.

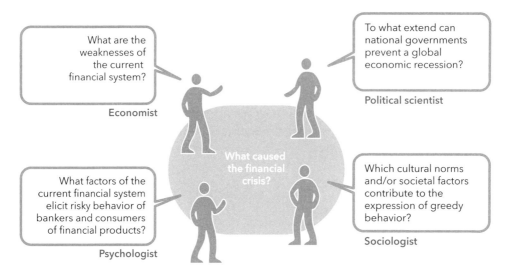

Figure 2 Different perspectives on the causes of the financial crisis

The previous examples illustrate that knowledge is, to a large extent, generated within separate disciplines (see also box 1). Consequently, in interdisciplinary research we need these disciplines to provide insights into different aspects of our research problem. So, before we turn the focus to interdisciplinarity, it is essential to understand what an academic discipline is. For this, it is useful to understand the origins of academic disciplines, as well as their development. In the following chapter, we define the academic discipline before providing an overview of the discipline's inception and expansion throughout the science system and beyond. This is followed by a definition of the concept of interdisciplinarity and important related concepts (chapter 4). Chapter 5 focuses on the importance of complexity as the driving force behind interdisciplinarity, and provides an overview of the different manifestations of complexity. Finally, chapter 6 provides a description of the integration of disciplinary knowledge to produce new, interdisciplinary insights (see the example below on an interdisciplinary theory on poverty), which is the key feature of interdisciplinary research.

Box 1

An interdisciplinary theory on poverty

Eldar Shafir and Sendhil Mullainathan, respectively Professor of Psychology at Princeton and Professor of Economics at Harvard, developed an interdisciplinary theory on poverty. Their theory, published in the book *Scarcity – Why Having Too Little Means So Much*, was praised both in and outside academia.

The starting point for their research was the finding that poor people generally make bad decisions. Compared to middle-class people, poor people eat less healthily (even when healthy food is made available to them), take out loans with high interest rates more often, and are generally bad at taking long-term effects into consideration. However, as Shafir said: "No one was studying why poor people are making these bad decisions" (E. Shafir, pers. comm., 12 December 2013).

Shafir and Mullainathan started to connect findings from their disciplines. They found that the bad decisions poor people make are actually well researched in psychology. For example, poor people were discounting the future and showed loss aversion in their decisions, two effects known from research on decision-making. The question the researchers then investigated was: Why are poor people more prone to these effects than others?

▼

In their experiments, they found that psychological traits like bad character or low intelligence could not explain why poor people made more bad decisions than people with more financial resources. Instead, Shafir and Mullainathan came up with another explanation: It is often a person's context that dictates whether someone can make a good decision. Shafir again: "Slowly came the realization that many of the mistakes made by the poor are caused by poverty itself."

In their book, the researchers explain that when someone experiences scarcity – whether it is a lack of money, friends or time – this shortage 'captures' that person's mind. Her mind will intentionally and unintentionally deal with scarcity, and this leaves less cognitive capacity for other things, such as making a good decision.

2 What is science?
A brief philosophy of science

2.1 What is science?

In the previous chapter we quoted philosopher of science Karl Popper, who contended that solving a problem often requires the integration of insights that pertain to different subject matters or disciplines. Popper observes a certain tension between the way that scientific disciplines are organized and how problems present themselves. Indeed, interdisciplinary research is a way to overcome this tension and to organize scientific research in such a way that it is not impeded by the organizational structure of the sciences itself. Since it is important to understand both the value and the limitations of this organizational structure, we need to briefly reflect on what science is and does. In other words: let us reflect on some basic ingredients of science, the way philosophers of science do. There are many ingredients that appear to be familiar enough, though perhaps not easy to understand, such as theory, concept, fact, hypothesis, explanation, inference, induction, deduction, and so on. Given the limitations of this handbook, we will only pay attention to a few of these and recommend you to look elsewhere for a more comprehensive introduction to the philosophy of science.

Scientists work hard to understand the world or reality, in much the same way as lay persons do. In fact, scientists cannot help but do this by building on the same pillars as we all have to. They have to rely upon sense perception in order to draw upon information about the world available and they have to use reasoning in order to draw the right conclusions about this information and to avoid mistakes. Nonetheless, if one reads scientific texts, it immediately becomes apparent that there are striking differences between scientific and lay efforts to reach an understanding of reality. Scientists do not usually rely on just their senses as lay persons do, but rather use a variety of instruments to perceive more, smaller, larger, and different objects than lay persons do: microscopes, structured interviews, telescopes, fMRI scanners, validated questionnaires, participatory observations, archive research, and so on. Similarly, their reasoning and arguments are often quite different from those of lay persons, as they work with rather specific concepts, propositions, formulas, figures, tables, and schemes and tend to strictly follow the laws of logic in connecting those. Put differently, they work with large and complex collections of symbols, all arranged in a quite particular structure.

Apart from the fact that scientists rely upon sense perception and reasoning in ways that are not common to the average lay person, but use quite specific instruments and methods, there is another fact that is peculiar to how scientists operate. One of the greatest scientists, Isaac Newton, once wrote in a letter to a colleague that "If I have seen further, it is by standing on the shoulders of giants." This remark reflects how scientists build upon each other's work, aim to put each other's work to the test, to expand the knowledge that others have produced, to use that knowledge in new applications, or to prove that their colleague's conclusions are not correct and that adjustments are required. In other words, much more than lay persons, a scientist is expected to be well informed about the relevant insights, results, instruments, and methods that other scientists have been and are using – relevant for answering the questions that the scientist is asking. Obviously, what is relevant for answering a particular question is often not easy to determine: a connection to a previously-held irrelevant factor might be established when new research has been executed and new instruments and methods have been developed, for example.

Employing highly elaborate forms of sense perception and reasoning, and building upon the relevant work of other scientists: these are important features that distinguish the scientists' acquisition of knowledge from the way lay persons operate. We can elucidate these features by looking at the figure below, which presents what is called the 'empirical cycle' or the 'Science Cycle': a process that represents how scientists go about when acquiring knowledge.

2.2   Moving through the Science Cycle

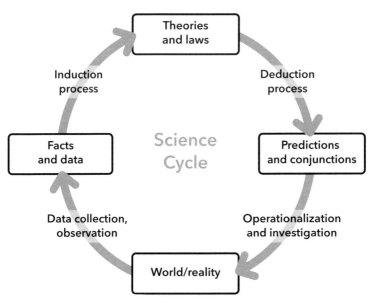

Figure 3   The Science Cycle, consisting of four processes, connecting four components - together providing a (somewhat simplified) representation of science as an ongoing process. Note that reasoning and sense perception are present, albeit in specific ways.

Theories and laws

The top of the Science Cycle (figure 3) consists of the most important component of science; that is to say, theories and laws. A theory consists of concepts, principles, ideas, or statements that together provide a comprehensive background or framework within which other ingredients of science are located. Familiar examples of theories are the theory of relativity, the theory of evolution, the behaviorist theory of learning, the structuralist theory of meaning, or the theory of plate tectonics.

In general, a theory offers a framework that usually captures the result of years of studies by numerous scientific colleagues, who have accumulated a wealth of facts and insights into a particular phenomenon. The theory offers elements that can be used to explain and predict phenomena that belong to the scope of the theory. If phenomena are complex, such as cognitive or social phenomena, it is likely that multiple theories are applicable to specific features of such phenomena: genetic, developmental, social, and geographical features might all be somehow relevant and might require interdisciplinary integration for a robust prediction and explanation, as we will learn in part 2. It is important to realize that there is a difference between the areas of research with regard to the prevalence and importance of specific theories. Physics is dominated by a few theories and a host of specific laws connected to those theories, while in the social sciences and humanities there are many competing theories but also many insights that have not been published in terms of a 'theory'. Given the fact that social, cultural, and historical phenomena are very complex and dynamic, this lesser prominence of theories in those domains should not be surprising, as such phenomena can usually be partly elucidated from multiple perspectives.

In many – though not in all – cases, we consider laws as part of a theory: for example, the law of gravity and several laws of motion belong to the theory of classical mechanics formulated by Newton. Somewhat differently, the Mendelian laws of inheritance are now part of the theory of classical genetics. Note that laws of inheritance have a probabilistic character, which distinguishes them from laws from classical mechanics and many other laws. Indeed, in the life, the social, and the human sciences such probabilistic laws are more prevalent because of the more multi-causal nature of phenomena in their domains. This also underlines the importance of distinguishing between correlative relations and causal relations: as long as we do not really know what causal mechanisms are involved, we should be cautious about interpreting probabilistic relations.

Deduction and developing predictions & conjunctions

As mentioned earlier, besides sense perception, reasoning is crucial for scientists, and deduction and induction are the most prominent reasoning processes involved in science. A scientist who wants to add to a body of knowledge will start by offering new predictions from a particular theory, or from the combination of two different theories – predictions that have, until now, not been formulated or tested. Such predictions are formulated by a particular logical reasoning process, called deduction.

Through deduction, one can derive specific statements from general ones. For example, the theory of classical mechanics implies that a heavy body exerts a force on other bodies. From this, it can be logically deduced that the earth exerts a force on the moon and vice versa. It cannot be logically deduced from this theory that all humans are mortal. The latter statement can instead be correctly deduced from a theory that describes how organisms decay and die over time. There are sound and unsound ways in which deduction can be done and it can happen that scientists make incorrect deductions, which will inevitably seriously flaw their research. In the case of alcohol and aggression, the scientist may deduce a specific prediction from the combination of a specific cognitive neuroscientific theory about how a particular brain process constitutes a person's emotional response with a biochemical theory about how alcohol has an impact on certain neurochemical processes in the brain. This novel combination of theories might lead him to offer a new detailed prediction regarding how alcohol use might lead to more aggressive responses. In the case of the interdisciplinary study of poverty, researchers had to consider whether their integrated insights into the socio-economic and psychological effects of poverty could be correctly deduced and were consistent with the existing theories on poverty. The process of deduction in humanities research is not always equally clear, as in physics or cognitive science, as phenomena in that domain tend to be determined by more than just a single set of factors. Nonetheless, when a humanities scholar aims to interpret a particular symbol or painting, she will still present a relevant knowledge base from which it might be deduced that the object under scrutiny can be interpreted in a specific way.

Often, one can find the term 'hypothesis' used interchangeably with 'prediction', yet the two are not identical. A hypothesis offers a specific explanation or insight into a phenomenon that can be put to the test and is based upon a scientist's expertise, rather than upon a specific set of data. Scientists then often proceed to compare a 'null hypothesis' – according to which the conjectured explanatory relation does not exist – with their 'alternative hypothesis'. Such educated guesses are indispensable in science, yet should be distinguished from predictions or conjectures that rely more specifically upon already existing data.

Operationalization and investigation of reality

The third component of the Science Cycle refers to the world or reality. Before a scientist can put his prediction to the test, she needs to think creatively about a reliable way to do this. It is one thing to deduce from the existing body of knowledge that there must be a connection between alcohol use and a person's responses; it is quite another and complex thing to develop an experiment and instrument to investigate this in a precise way. The scientist must think of how to operationalize her prediction and what investigation might be sufficient to study the operationalized prediction. Such an investigation may require experimentation, but it might also require different forms of study, such as archive research or in-depth interviews with subjects. That said, in order for other scientists to be able to check and control the findings of others, the operationalization must be such that it can be repeated and reproduced by others at other locations and times.

In the case of our example on the relation between alcohol and aggression, questions emerge such as: what are the relevant neurochemical compounds to be investigated? Are these compounds directly or indirectly affected by the influx of alcohol into the body? What brain areas are relevant and how can we find out whether these have any effects on a person's behavior? What instruments do we need to use to detect these effects, and what behavioral changes can we use as an indicator of aggression? Who might we use as guinea pigs for such experiments or observations, and what is the appropriate amount (ethically and health-wise) of alcohol that they should drink, in what period of time? What statistical methods can we use to analyze the data that our experiment might yield in order to determine whether its results are valid and significant? Comparable questions have to be answered by the humanities scholar or the social scientist who has developed a prediction or conjunction about, for example, the meaning of a particular symbol in the Renaissance, or the power relations that have influenced its meaning. The humanities scholar might want to operationalize her question by focusing on the use of such a symbol in paintings, which requires her to combine insights from plant iconology with those about Renaissance paintings to suggest a probable interpretation of the symbol at stake. The social scientist, in turn, might want to focus on a particular religious crisis and seek to understand this by employing a structuralist theory of power and combine it with insights about how, in that particular religion, social hierarchical relations are justified. In other words, humanities scholars and social scientists also need to determine how to relate general theories or previous insights into particular objects or events in order to understand the object of their investigation.

Data collection and observation and induction: Toward theories and laws

Having deduced from one or more theories a particular prediction or conjunction, and having operationalized these in such a way that a study or investigation of a particular object or event in the world is possible, the scientist will now be able to collect and observe certain results, data, or facts. Part of the collection and observation of facts also entails, of course, their analysis; for example, the statistical analysis of data on individuals' alcohol use combined with the data on their response changes. At this stage, sense perception is involved, but you will realize that this perception is facilitated in crucial ways by processes such as theorizing, reasoning, operationalization, and experimentation and by the use of specific methods and instruments (e.g. computer software to run your statistical tests), which have been developed over time via similar processes in previous decades or even centuries by fellow scientists. Indeed, philosophers of science often refer to this entanglement of observation with the other processes of the Science Cycle by referring to the 'theory-ladenness' of observations.

In short, the perception that scientists rely upon is, in many ways, very different from the perception that lay persons refer to when they mention their own observations as support for their statements. Lay persons sometimes believe that there are 'naked facts' that inevitably lead any sensible person to a particular conclusion. You will probably understand by now that even unscientific perceptions are dependent upon the knowledge and beliefs that someone has. Most adults will agree that the perception that the earth is flat is an illusion caused by the fact that it is nearly impossible to perceive, with the naked eye, the slight curvature of the earth – yet children might still insist on the earth being flat. Yet, even if a sensible lay person has reliably witnessed a series of events, she may still be mistaken in the conclusion that she draws from it. This brings us to the last process involved in the Science Cycle – induction.

As mentioned at the beginning, science builds upon sense perception, logically sound reasoning processes, and the accumulated results of previous generations of scientists. When we started to discuss the figure of the Science Cycle, we began with the most important component of science', that is to say, the theories, concepts, and insights that are characteristic of science. Yet, where do these theories, concepts, and insights come from, and how did they emerge? Surely, they must somehow be founded on facts or on data. It is difficult to give a straight answer to this question for two reasons. One reason is that by entering the Science Cycle, each scientist builds upon the work of her predecessors, which also implies – as we noted above – that all scientifically acquired facts and observations are 'theory-laden'. It is impossible to do science and to gather data without somehow relying upon previously developed theories, as these have contributed to the development of the instruments, procedures, analytical techniques, and other elements of data acquisition. So theories do not just emerge from data alone, but are being built – perhaps indirectly – on other theories as well.

And there is a second reason why theories and concepts are not merely derived from facts or data and it has to do with the problem of induction. Alongside deduction, induction is the most important logical reasoning process that scientists use in their work, but it is far more complicated than deduction. For example, there are many ways in which one can deduce multiple particular statements in a perfectly logical way from a general statement or theory: if all animals are mortal, for example, one can deduce that birds are mortal, and that mammals are mortal, and that Socrates is mortal, and so on. Making an inference in the other direction with induction, however, is never perfect or completely reliable. If, for example, one has found that birds reproduce sexually, and that mammals reproduce sexually, and that Socrates has reproduced sexually, it is still not correct to infer from this that all animals reproduce sexually. Indeed, further investigation would reveal that not only quite a few plants reproduce asexually, but also some insects, amphibians, and reptiles do so via unfertilized eggs. Unfortunately, inducing a generally valid theory from a limited set of facts or data is logically never completely warranted and therefore always tricky.

Indeed, any data set is inevitably limited as the future or past may, here or elsewhere in the universe, yield unexpected facts. The scientists in our example may, at some point, have found data to support their general theory that alcohol abuse tends to lead to increased aggression in humans, but it has been discovered more recently that persons with a particular genetic mutation are able to decompose alcohol much better than most people. Their induction has turned out to be flawed and they will have to adjust and specify their theory, making it less general, by accounting for the exception that scientists are now aware of.

Nonetheless, if we want to expand our knowledge we cannot do so without using induction at some point. Yet, it is important to realize the inevitable risk involved in induction and to develop counter-measures that help to mitigate that risk. We will deal with such a counter-measure shortly. Before doing so, it is appropriate to mention here the lesson that the previously quoted philosopher of science Karl Popper drew from this precarious nature of induction. He insisted that since induction is always precarious and we can never infer a true general statement with utter certainty from observed facts, scientists should give up proving a theory true and instead aim to disprove incorrect theories. In Popper's words: they should devote their efforts to 'falsification' instead of 'verification'. For such a falsification or proof of falseness we only need a single observation, as that single observation is sufficient to teach us the important lesson that our current theory is not yet adequate. Generally, scientists do not comply entirely with Popper's advice and tend to adopt both strategies, i.e. they check whether a particular theory might easily be falsified or disproved, but they also seek to confirm (another) theory by gathering further support for it.

Some final remarks: Pluralism and assumptions

Popper's critique of verification points to an important insight: merely repeating the same experiment or investigation over and over again might yield a huge collection of data yet still fail to prove a theory's truth. Conducting a more robust scientific investigation requires the use of a plurality of methods and theories. As mentioned above, given the complex and dynamic nature of many phenomena, a single theory is often not sufficient to understand these completely. For the relation between alcohol and aggression we have to combine genetic, social scientific, and psychological theories, for example. Similarly, our methods of investigation should be diverse. This means that if the connection between alcohol use and aggressive responses in our group of subjects is founded not just on investigations focusing on the psychological level, but also on the group level and on the genetic level, our inference – or induction – to a causal connection is more trustworthy than if it rested upon a single research method and its associated theories. Not surprisingly, interdisciplinary research by its very nature implies theoretical and methodological pluralism. This brings its own difficulties but usually also yields more robust results than monism does.

Finally, it is important to realize that although scientists need to be much more explicit and articulate about the theories and insights they use, and about the reasoning behind their predictions and conclusions, scientists still silently assume a lot when doing all this. Such assumptions are often based upon very specific expertise pertinent to a scientific field, but they can also have a much vaguer background. Implicit assumptions are associated with many features in science:

assumptions can pertain to the applicability of measuring instruments, to the number and nature of causes of a phenomenon, to the validity of a scientific conclusion to a domain of reality, and so on. For instance, most scientists nowadays silently assume that the universe will behave tomorrow according to the same laws as yesterday and today: if they did not believe this, their research would perhaps only be relevant for explaining today's phenomena. An assumption that has turned out to be false since the discovery of epigenetics is the assumption that DNA is the only carrier of inherited information across generations. More specifically, cognitive scientists have assumed for a long time that their main reliance upon Western psychology students as subjects would not have an impact upon the general validity of their studies of visual perception. This assumption has now been challenged, as it appears that socio-cultural differences do have an impact upon perception. Acceptation of this assumption could have far-reaching consequences for cognitive science and psychology, but there are understandable reservations against this.

Interdisciplinarians should particularly acknowledge scientific pluralism and the importance of assumptions. As interdisciplinary research consists of integrating insights from different sciences, notwithstanding their theoretical and methodological differences, understanding and recognizing the relevance of pluralism is a good starting point. Similarly, implicit assumptions can often prevent scientists from collaborating or learning from each other, while articulating these assumptions might facilitate this. The rejection of the assumption of DNA being the only carrier of inherited information with the discovery of epigenetic inheritance, for example, suggested that geneticists, ethologists, and developmental scientists could work together to explain the transmission of environmental stress or anxiety across generations, which, in turn, might be related to alcohol abuse. Similarly, recognizing that Western psychology students might not be representative of the global population in all respects has led to fruitful collaborations between cognitive scientists, cultural anthropologists, and sociologists.

With these remarks on pluralism and assumptions, we close this brief philosophical discussion on what science is. The ingredients that have been discussed in this chapter will return in what is to come below. But first we will discuss what disciplines are, since we are not doing 'science' in a general sense; rather, we are doing physics or cognitive science or history or European studies, and so on: science is organized in terms of disciplines.

3 The disciplines

Before we introduce the concept of interdisciplinarity, we must first explain what an academic discipline is. It is, however, not easy to give an exact definition, as disciplines are often fragmented, heterogeneous, and subject to change. Furthermore, academic disciplines have always influenced each other and have sometimes incorporated elements of one another, further complicating the formulation of a unifying definition. These complicating factors in defining a discipline are illustrated in the next paragraph on the history of disciplines.

3.1 Academic disciplines: A brief history

Throughout history, scientists and philosophers have defined disciplines in quite different ways. An influential and traditional view lingers behind Popper's contention that scientists are not 'students of some subject matter' that would have some 'boundaries'. It implicitly refers to a traditional view of scientific disciplines as being organized around distinct domains of reality. A discipline that has been admired by many in ancient and modern times and that is organized in such a way around a distinct and separate domain of reality is mathematics, which has also been considered very successful in terms of the quality and certainty of the knowledge it generates and its growth. Mathematics was held to be exemplary because mathematicians can more or less create their own 'subject matter' by providing definitions, axioms, and postulates upon which an elaborate geometry can be built. As long as one makes logically sound deductions from these 'elements of geometry' (in Euclid's terms), one can gain new insights that are definitely true and reliable. This example is still influential, also outside the field of mathematics, for example in econometrics and in quantum physics.

The influential scientist and philosopher of science Aristotle held that we could apply a similar approach to knowledge to subject matters outside of mathematics. Aristotle argued that the domain of disciplines like physics, biology, or psychology is equally determined by the nature and properties of their respective subject matter. Consequently, explanations pertaining to those disciplines must also refer to the defining factors of their domain. In the case of explanations in physics, for example, these should somehow be related to the nature of matter, its properties and its movements. Biologists explain their phenomena by eventually referring to the defining properties of organisms and their respective environments.

This account of the organization of science and scientific disciplines has been influential for many centuries. What is positive about such a view of science and of scientific disciplines is that it helped to recognize that scientific knowledge is possible subject matters other than mathematics alone, allowing empirical observations and even experimental results to play their part. What is problematic, however, is that the borders between defined 'subject matters' appear to be strict and that connections between these different domains and the scientific disciplines targeting them are not obvious. Only in a limited sense, according to this view, can a mathematician or a physicist explain a biological phenomenon; namely, to the extent that this phenomenon can be described in quantitative terms or involves matter and movement. Accordingly, those other disciplines cannot really explain the biological phenomenon as such.

There are several reasons why this picture of disciplines being organized around definable and distinct subject matters or domains of reality was gradually abandoned. For brevity's sake, we will mention only four. For a long time it has been common for many scientists to work in more than just a single domain or discipline. Naturally, they would often apply the theories and research methods of a particular domain to another domain, as it could yield valuable results and therefore question the separation between those domains. Another reason is that the exemplary status of mathematics for science in general was contested by many scientists: in particular, with the growing importance of scientific experimentation and observation, the prominence of deductive reasoning from definitions and axioms waned. Instead, scientists and philosophers of science came to realize that most scientific disciplines entail a plurality of theories and methods, which makes it increasingly difficult to strictly separate them. Third, from the end of the nineteenth century, increasing specialization challenged the initial idea that a scientific discipline is organized around a particular and distinct subject matter or domain of reality. Indeed, how should one understand the fact that the original domains of mathematics, physics, biology, psychology and so on turned out to be further subdivided into many subdomains like particle physics, microbiology, or developmental psychology? Finally, and in contrast to the previous development, particularly in the twentieth century, the collaboration between disciplines and the emergence of new 'interdisciplines' intensified. There are several reasons for this development, as we will consider below.

Given these developments and the erosion of the traditional view of how a scientific discipline is determined, alternatives have been proposed over the years. A very influential general account of science is given by Thomas Kuhn, emphasizing the bumpy history of both science and of our understanding of what science is. In his *Structure of Scientific Revolutions* from 1962, he introduced the notion of 'paradigm', with which he aims to characterize a particular scientific discipline at a given time. According to this account, a scientific discipline is not determined by definitions, axioms and postulates that determine its contents and the methods that are adequate for handling these contents. In contrast, a paradigm refers in a much looser sense to a set of assumptions, values, methods, theories and practices that are shared by a certain community of scientists. This rich notion allowed Kuhn to emphasize the fact that a particular discipline is not just constituted by specific contents and methods. Instead, it implies that also social factors, values and practices matter, like there being a community of colleagues who together share practices and ideas about their field. An important consequence of this broader notion is that there may, at times, be different communities within one and the same discipline that subscribe to different paradigms about it. Indeed, this situation implies that the term 'discipline' has inevitably lost some of its appeal given the lack of consensus about its contents, methods, practices and such like. Such rifts within a discipline can be found in all fields; as the history of science demonstrates, revolutionary ideas are initially often met with much resistance and can shake up any discipline. Well-known cases are Galileo, Darwin, Marx, Freud, and Einstein, whose revolutionary ideas were recognized quickly by some colleagues, whereas others would stick to the old 'paradigms' and warn against those 'attacks'. After a while, however, the shortcomings of the traditional contents and practices were more generally recognized, as was the value of the new contender. In several cases, a so-called 'paradigm-shift' occurred within those disciplines, which was then followed by a period of 'normal science' during which many colleagues shared the new paradigm. However, in other cases a peculiar mix of the old and new paradigms would develop over time or different paradigms would continue to co-exist.

The lesson of this brief history should be that even though we still use the notion of a scientific 'discipline', we should be careful in assuming that this term refers to a distinct and well-definable entity. On the contrary, we have seen that a discipline nowadays is considered to be both internally pluralistic and no longer separable from other disciplines in a neat sense. Once we recognize this, it may help us to understand how interdisciplinary and transdisciplinary collaborations can be achieved and how they can differ from each other. Some collaborations may be based on shared concepts, others on shared methods or theories, and yet others might share some values about what useful knowledge amounts to. Importantly, scientists should be aware that their collaborative efforts may still leave differences intact regarding their views about the ingredients of reality (ontology), about true and reliable knowledge (epistemology), and about what are important and unimportant questions (including moral questions). The challenge for interdisciplinarians is to be aware of this fact and to articulate and communicate about these questions in order to avoid them impeding their research.

3.2   Our definition of a discipline

From the brief history above, it becomes clear that it is quite difficult to assemble a set of criteria that a field of inquiry must meet before it can be called a discipline. Let us nonetheless make an attempt to do so. We define a discipline as a field of science with a particular object of research and a corresponding body of accumulated specialist knowledge. This knowledge is effectively organized by and expressed through theories, concepts, and assumptions inclusive of its discipline-specific terminologies and technical language. Furthermore, a discipline has its own specific research methods and has an institutional manifestation (usually at universities). The last criterion is especially important, since the reproduction of a discipline from generation to generation typically requires an educational component (Krishnan, 2009).

We can say that academic disciplines are products of the way scientists in the same field organize their knowledge to gain a better understanding of the world. However, concurring with Popper, we should realize that the disciplinary structure does not provide us with a perfect representation of our world, and the boundaries between and focus of interest within disciplines change over time as we have argued above. The current division of domains of knowledge into academic disciplines has its roots largely in recent history. This division was developed mainly in response to the growth and growing importance of scientific activities and scientific education. Along with the rapid growth of scientific communities – in universities, academies, commercial firms and other associations – from the nineteenth century onwards, a quickly growing body of knowledge was produced. In order to organize all this, classifications and other systems were proposed (Abma, 2011; Frodeman, Klein & Mitcham, 2010).

Despite their relatively recent inception, the disciplines that emerged have been very dominant in the organization of the science system and the application of its results to society. The development of disciplines has had advantages for the development of knowledge, mainly because disciplines allow for the production and transfer of more specific and in-depth knowledge. Laws and regularities become most apparent when scientists study them in isolation from other features of a research object. This enables scientists to devote themselves entirely to a particular cause and its effect. In many disciplines, reductionist science (which holds that a complex system can be understood by research into its constituting parts, as will be further explained in chapter 4) has been very successful at accomplishing this. For example, it enabled scientists to identify the primary laws of nature. However, in the twentieth century, scientists started to realize that many (but not all) phenomena and problems could not be understood by only studying their simplest parts and behavior in such isolation. The 'whole is more than the sum of its parts' logic has evolved into an anti-reductionist catchphrase and has been proven correct in numerous fields of science like biology, medicine, and sociology (Mitchell, 2009). We want to stress, however, that both reductionist and holistic science are of value, depending on the type of problems studied. Interdisciplinary research, therefore, usually involves both reductionism (drawing insights from various disciplines) and holism (integrating insights from various disciplines into a more comprehensive understanding).

As knowledge is generated, stored, and transferred within separate disciplines, disciplines also perform functions of socialization. That is, students of a certain discipline learn not only about the subject matter of that particular discipline, but also about the customs, most common methods, conventions, and assumptions that are inherent to that discipline. Through the process of sharing these ideas with students upon their introduction to the discipline, through education, and through peer review of publications in academic journals and books, the disciplines are continually assessed and reinforced. In short, through the institutionalization of disciplines, a structured system of science has been created in which the quality of knowledge is monitored and guaranteed. However, this system may also limit cross-disciplinary innovations (Abma, 2011; Frodeman et al., 2010).

Funding agencies, which until recently have been largely responsible for maintaining the traditional division into disciplines, increasingly stress the societal relevance of research as well as prompting for a more inclusive, hence interdisciplinary mode of research. Consequently, a new mode of application-oriented research is emerging, in addition to traditional fundamental academic research. In other words, not only is the science system growing in size, but its structure and functioning are undergoing developments as the locus of research, the patterns of collaboration, and the aims of the scientific enterprise are subject to change (Abma, 2011).

3.3 Classification of academic disciplines

Over time, different classifications of disciplines have emerged. In general, we distinguish three major groups of disciplines: the natural sciences, the social sciences, and the humanities. The subject matter of the natural sciences is the natural world. The natural sciences include disciplines such as mathematics, physics, chemistry, and biology, as shown in green in figure 4. The social sciences focus on human behavior and society. Examples include sociology, psychology, political science, and economics, as depicted in red. The humanities, on the other hand, study the products of mankind and consist of disciplines such as literature, history, and philosophy, which is shown in yellow. Note that there are several disciplines, like logic and mathematics, which figure in all groups of disciplines. An overview of academia's major disciplines is displayed in figure 4.

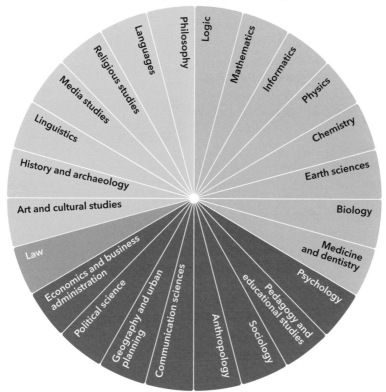

Figure 4   An overview of academic disciplines as presented by the University of Amsterdam

One can identify sub-disciplines within each of the major disciplines. For example, there are numerous specialized sub-disciplines or branches within the field of biology. Some are classified according to the level of organization they study, such as molecular biology, cell biology, or ecology. Other sub-disciplines are characterized by the type of organisms they study (e.g. botany and zoology) or their focus on a practical application (e.g. conservation biology). An overview of the various branches that can be distinguished within biology is displayed in figure 5. As their names reveal, some of the branches already combine insights from various disciplines. For example, biochemistry combines biology and chemistry, cognitive neuroscience combines cognition and neuroscience, and biocomputing combines biology and computational sciences. Such sub-disciplines can be called 'inter-disciplines', which might over time develop into separate disciplines, conforming to the features of a discipline mentioned above.

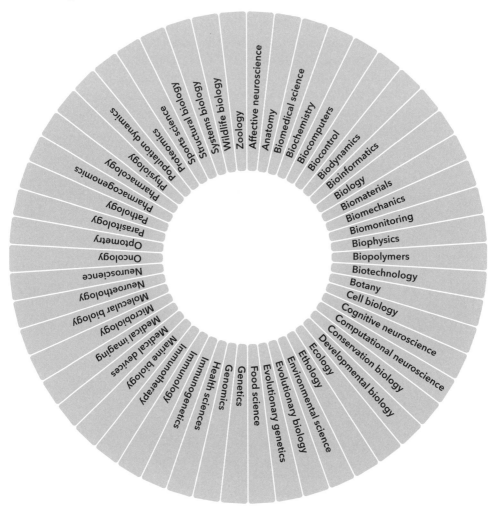

Figure 5   The many branches of biology

4 Interdisciplinarity

Now that we know what academic disciplines are and how they emerged and developed, it is time to introduce interdisciplinarity. One of the most widely used and adequate definitions of interdisciplinarity comes from the National Academy of Sciences (2005):

> Interdisciplinary research is a mode of research in which an individual scientist or a team of scientists integrates information, data, techniques, tools, perspectives, concepts, and/or theories from two or more disciplines or bodies of specialized knowledge, with the objective to advance fundamental understanding or to solve problems whose solutions are beyond the scope of a single discipline or area of research practice.

Other definitions include those of Klein and Newell (1997), who define interdisciplinarity as "a process of answering a question, solving a problem, or addressing a topic that is too broad or complex to be dealt with adequately by a single discipline or profession [...] and draws on disciplinary perspectives and integrates their insights through construction of a more comprehensive perspective" (pp. 393-394). Interdisciplinarity has become a buzzword in scientific debates, and it has been identified by many research funding organizations in Europe and the United States as an important factor in future research. Although there is no single accepted definition of interdisciplinarity and the term is sometimes used interchangeably with multidisciplinarity and transdisciplinarity, it is important to distinguish and describe these three different manifestations of research.

The basic difference between these manifestations of research that spread beyond a discipline is the extent to which researchers aim for the integration or synthesis of (disciplinary) insights. Interdisciplinary research literally means research between disciplines, referring to the interaction of disciplines with each other. Indeed, the Social Science Research Council in New York, which first used the term 'interdisciplinary' around 1925, aimed to facilitate collaborations between the social scientific disciplines it did oversee (Klein, 1990). Such interaction may range from the mere communication and comparison of ideas, through the exchange of data, methods, and procedures, to the mutual integration of organizing concepts, theories, methodology, and epistemological principles. In multidisciplinary research, the subject under study is also approached from different angles, using different disciplinary perspectives. However, in that case neither the theoretical perspectives nor the findings of the various disciplines are integrated. Lastly, transdisciplinary research also involves actors from fields outside of the university, thereby allowing for the integration of academic and non-academic or experiential knowledge (Hirsch-Hadorn et al., 2008).

In this handbook, we will use the following definitions:
1   Multidisciplinary research is research that involves more than one discipline, but without integration. Results from the involved disciplines are compared and conclusions are subsequently drawn from each of the individual disciplines, but there is no integration of the disciplinary insights.
2   Interdisciplinary research is research in which relevant concepts, theories, and/ or methodologies from different academic disciplines, as well as the results or insights these disciplines generate, are integrated.
3   Transdisciplinary research occurs when researchers collaborate with stakeholders from outside the academic world. Knowledge from outside the academic world, as well as stakeholder values, is integrated with academic knowledge. Together, these insights determine what problem is studied and how this is done, and which interventions are selected to address the problem.

Figure 6 illustrates these different approaches to research.

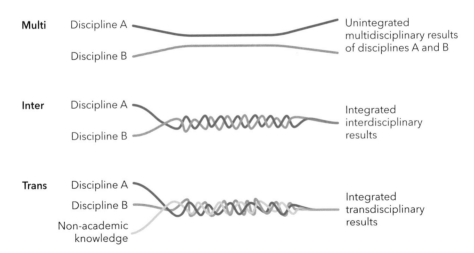

Figure 6   Multidisciplinarity, interdisciplinarity, and transdisciplinarity illustrated

Although in theory multi-, inter-, and transdisciplinarity can be distinguished, in practice researchers often switch between these approaches – sometimes within the same research project. For example, at the Dutch Research Institute for Transitions (DRIFT) researchers always go from trans- to inter- to multidisciplinarity (see the interview with DRIFT-director Dr. Derk Loorbach in chapter 13).
In the case of the alcohol and aggression research, scientists in a multidisciplinary team might shed light on the specific genetic and neurochemical and psychological

factors involved, often by conducting individually highly specialized disciplinary research. A further step then consists of the interdisciplinary integration of their insights by determining a specific genetic factor that modulates the neurochemical pathway along which alcohol affects an inhibitory process in subjects. This might then lead to a transdisciplinary research project involving alcoholics and their families, aimed at developing a socially robust intervention that prevents aggression.

5 Complexity: the main driving force behind interdisciplinarity

In the previous chapter, we defined multidisciplinarity and interdisciplinarity, but why and when would we need to employ an interdisciplinary research approach instead of a multidisciplinary or a monodisciplinary one? To answer this question, it is necessary to understand that a scientist may respond to several kinds of motivations or 'drivers' in undertaking interdisciplinary projects. The National Academy of Sciences (2005) identifies four drivers of interdisciplinary research: 1) The inherent complexity of nature and society; 2) The drive to explore basic research problems at the interfaces of disciplines; 3) The need to solve societal problems; and 4) The stimulus of generative technologies. Interestingly, these drivers share an important characteristic that cuts across disciplines: complexity. Complexity is widely recognized as one of the main themes in science today. As British physicist Stephen Hawking said: "This century is the century of complexity, and complexity and its associated technologies and theories of artificial life, agent-based models, self-organization and the science of networks will revolutionize the way science is done." Problems and phenomena that require an interdisciplinary approach all somehow show the characteristics of complex (adaptive) systems, which are explained in this chapter.

Before describing the drivers of interdisciplinary research as defined by the NAS and embraced by our Institute for Interdisciplinary Studies' approach, and consequently employed in this handbook, we need a basic understanding of complexity. This chapter explains complexity and related concepts and sets out its various manifestations, which can be translated into the drivers of interdisciplinary research. These drivers will be described later in this chapter. In the academic world, there is much debate about the definition of complexity. On the one hand, complexity science studies complex systems and their dynamics in a mathematical way; on the other hand, the notion of complexity is used in a broader sense. In the social sciences, complexity is also used to describe the inherent uncertainty of large-scale societal issues (such as 'wicked problems', which lack a definitive formulation or solution – these will be explained later on p. 39). It is important to note that interdisciplinary research in many cases addresses problems derived from complex systems, but does not necessarily study the dynamics of those systems. However, we think it is crucial to have an idea of the dynamics within complex systems when engaging in interdisciplinary research.

5.1 Complex (adaptive) systems

In complexity science, the objects of study are often defined as complex adaptive systems (CASs). CASs are "at the heart of many contemporary problems" (Holland, 2006). Systems as diverse as ecosystems, human consciousness, the immune system, stock markets, cities, and societies can be characterized as complex adaptive systems.

But what defines a CAS? There are four basic factors that are essential for a system to be classified as complex, as opposed to just being complicated. The first necessary condition is the presence of a collection of diverse 'agents'. The agents might be atoms, molecules, cells, football hooligans, or multinationals, depending on the complex system that is studied. Second, these agents have to be interconnected and their behavior and actions have to be interdependent; in other words, the agents must form a network. The third key criterion is that the collection of agents tends to self-organize as a result of feedback and feed-forward loops between agents. And finally, the agents must be able to adapt to change (in the local or global environment) or to learn (Holland, 2006; Levin, 1998; Page, 2010). As a result, CASs are unpredictable.

As a consequence of the diversity in connections and interactions between individual agents, CASs often behave in non-linear ways (meaning the output is not necessarily proportional to the input) and can therefore shift from one state to another or suddenly collapse. However, CASs also have a certain buffer capacity, which makes them resilient to change and thereby robust. Furthermore, CASs are characterized by emergent phenomena, i.e. phenomena that can be observed at a more global, macro level and which typically cannot be predicted from or reduced to the properties of the constituent elements (at a lower, micro level). These are emergent properties that arise through (self-organizing) local interactions and feedback and feed-forward loops.

This idea contrasts with the classical reductionist perspective, by which nature can be (best) understood by reducing or decomposing its processes into elementary building blocks that, in turn, can be analyzed in isolation from other components. For example, think of the human brain: Neurons are merely cells passing on signals to one another; yet, an interconnected network of billions of them gives rise to the brain's emerging property of consciousness. Another example is the order of a city, with the organization of its infrastructure, its countless daily flows of goods, and people living their daily lives: It functions, even though there is no central planner (Page, 2010). It is important to note, however, that CAS theory typically ignores the role of human volition and values. Humans consciously pay attention to the influence they exert on their own higher levels of organization, such as groups, societies, or sometimes even the species as a whole. Moreover, they are capable of altering their effects on those higher levels of organization. Examples of individuals working together to do this include governments, NGOs, and international organizations, such as the European Union and the United Nations. However, according to typical CAS theories, all macro-level phenomena are the result of emergence: They are produced by the system, rather than by collective human intentionality. This is important to bear in mind when studying social phenomena.

In such studies, CASs should be used in combination with macro-level social science analyses (W.H. Newell, pers. comm., 3 December 2013).

It is important to note that there is a difference between complex and complicated. A system can be complicated without being complex. Take, for example, a wristwatch. This is a complicated system, but we cannot define it as being complex. This is because the behavior of a watch is linear, and therefore more or less predictable. Moreover, a watch is not very robust. If we lift a hammer and smash a watch, it will not resist the impact, nor will it adapt after it has been smashed. A corporation, on the other hand, is complex. When you decide to retire from your job at an organization, the corporation will, conceivably, adapt to this change, for example by hiring someone else. In other words, it will not stop functioning. Therefore, a corporation is complex as it exerts robustness. In addition, a watch does not show emergent properties once it is put together: The movements of its pointers, shafts, and cogs can perfectly be described with the physics that apply to its parts in isolation from each other and no completely unexpected properties emerge from their interactions.

Now, you might be asking why addressing complexity is so important. The answer is that we are living in complex times. Whether we like it or not, complexity is the inescapable reality. For example, the world has become more complex, mostly because of increased interconnectedness, at least on social, economic, and political levels. Some 10,000 years ago, people lived in groups relatively isolated from others in different geographical regions, depending only on their own community. In today's world, however, we have global markets that connect companies and consumers all over the world. Global markets are both highly interdependent and adaptable to change, and can thus be classified as complex. In addition, this increased social complexity has also had repercussions in the physical and biological world. As a result of global interconnectedness, biological species can spread rapidly over the planet. In addition, problems such as climate change and biodiversity loss are affecting the environment on a global scale. It is through scientific research that we have become more aware of the physical world's complexity. Whereas complicated problems can often be adequately understood by separate disciplines, complex problems need to be addressed interdisciplinarily (see for example the interdisciplinary theory on complex systems in box 2).

Box 2

An interdisciplinary theory on complex systems:
Tipping points

Ecologist Marten Scheffer has done extensive research on the sudden shift from a clear to a turbid water state in shallow lakes. Building on the work of Canadian ecologist C.S. Holling, who first coined the idea of ecological resilience, Scheffer investigated the underlying mechanisms causing the sudden shift in shallow lakes. One of the factors triggering a regime shift is nutrient loading. Increasing nutrient concentrations have no or little effect on a shallow lake until a critical threshold is passed, after which the lake suddenly shifts toward a turbid state. Both the clear and the turbid state show a certain amount of stability or resilience to change, as a consequence of negative feedback mechanisms. For example, in the clear state, the lake ecosystem is dominated by macrophytes (aquatic plants), which can only live in the presence of light. The macrophytes themselves maintain the clear state by holding together sediments. By contrast, the turbid state is characterized by dominance of algae. In addition, because of the lack of macrophytes, sediments are not held together, further contributing to the turbid state. Thus, both states are self-stabilizing, but external factors such as high nutrient levels may push the system over a tipping point and cause a regime shift (Scheffer, Carpenter, Foley, Folke & Walker, 2001).

Such tipping points and alternative dynamic equilibria (i.e. the clear or the turbid lake in the example above) can be found not only in ecosystems, but also in a variety of other complex systems. In fact, we see such abrupt changes all around us. Stock market crashes, the sudden collapse of past societies, epileptic seizures, migraine attacks, and the civil uprisings that erupted in the Arab world in 2010 and 2011 during the so-called Arab Spring are but a few examples of these tipping points.

Most of the examples above cannot be researched as easily as shallow lakes, since they are more complex. Since we have seen such sudden changes in history, however, the theory of tipping points provides valuable insights, also for disciplines other than ecology.

Despite the inherent difficulty in defining complexity, we can now begin to identify two of the main drivers of interdisciplinary research that were mentioned above (NAS 2005). The first is the inherent complexity of nature and society. Secondly, the NAS identifies the drive to explore basic research problems at the interfaces of disciplines as a driver. In addition, there is a need to solve societal problems, which accounts for the second driver that is more action-oriented. And lastly, the stimulus of generative technologies can be identified as a driver of interdisciplinarity.

Driver 1: The inherent complexity of nature and society

Problems concerning nature and society are inherently complex. Addressing such problems implies aiming to understand, for example, how the brain stores memories, how ecosystems can be resilient to change, how the immune system coordinates a defense reaction to a bacterial infection or how fragmented terrorist networks function. Of course, these questions might also arise in more fundamental research, without a direct aim of obtaining applicable results. Initiatives for interdisciplinary research are triggered not only by societal concern, but also by academic curiosity. This has created 'borderlands' between the disciplines, or new schools of thought, such as sociobiology and psycholinguistics

As the NAS puts it (2005, p. 30), a complex system such as climate change cannot be understood comprehensively per se "without considering the influence of the oceans, rivers, sea ice, atmospheric constituents, solar radiation, transport processes, land use, land cover, and other anthropogenic practices and feedback mechanisms that link this "system of subsystems" across scales of space and time." Understanding complex processes therefore depends on collecting insights from multiple disciplines. Both deep knowledge from monodisciplinary perspectives and expertise in their interdisciplinary integration are essential to address the fundamental questions that pertain to our reality. Collaboration across the natural sciences, social sciences, and humanities is required to answer such questions fully.

Driver 2: The drive to explore basic research problems at the interfaces of disciplines

Initiatives for more interdisciplinary research are triggered not only by societal concern, but also by scientific curiosity, by the wish to explore problems and questions that are located at the interface of disciplines. These borderlands between the disciplines are inhabited by new schools of thought, such as biochemistry, sociobiology, and neuroethics, which allow researchers to address previously difficult to answer questions and to pursue new topics. The exploration of the interfaces between disciplines challenges the know-how of the researchers and stimulates them to invite researchers from adjacent fields to collaborate and share their knowledge.

Driver 3: The need to solve societal problems

Today, more than ever, there is an expectation that scientific research will, in some way, contribute to solving important societal issues. This expectation exists because science and technology provide many of the techniques and tools that help society to cope with major current and future challenges. These include themes such as food, water, health, energy, and globalization. Science is often seen as a 'troubleshooter' when it comes to solving complex problems. However, it is important to realize that any intervention in such complex phenomena might lead to unexpected changes of the complex system. Indeed, there is usually a bi-directional relationship between technological fixes and societal problems, as technological fixes often create new problems in addition to providing solutions. Some demonstrations of such a bi-directional relationship are, for example, the impact of artificial fertilizers on water pollution, the increase of automotive transportation and subsequent highway deaths, the development of life-supporting technologies and pressing issues of euthanasia, and the growth of urban areas and related loss of rural land and natural habitat. Such societal problems qualify as wicked problems.

Wicked problems lack a definitive formulation or, more importantly, a solution and are complex by nature. They are the opposite of tame problems, which can be tackled with traditional (disciplinary) science. Wicked problems require additional considerations compared to tame problems and often necessitate multiple perspectives to understand the problem and eventually suggest solutions. Examples of wicked problems include climate change, poverty, the HIV epidemic, healthcare, and social injustice. Wicked problems essentially share nine characteristics (adapted with some modifications from Rittel & Webber, 1973):

- There is no definitive description for a wicked problem. Because of the complex nature of wicked problems, it is impossible to give an exact description. Too many factors underlying the problem influence each other. As a result, the formulation of a wicked problem is in fact a problem in itself!
- Because solving the problem is more or less the same as defining it, there is no stopping rule. There is no definitive solution, just as there is no definitive description.
- Solutions to wicked problems are neither true, nor false. They are rather defined in terms of better or worse. For instance, a solution might be qualified as 'satisfying'.
- There is no (immediate or ultimate) test of a solution to a wicked problem.
- Every solution to a wicked problem is a 'one-shot operation'. Since every attempt to solve a wicked problem affects the underlying system, it inevitably alters the initial problem. Trial and error is not possible: in fact, every trial counts.
- There is no enumerable set of possible solutions to a wicked problem. Moreover, there is no complete overview of permissible or inadmissible solutions.
- Each wicked problem is essentially unique. There are no definite classes of wicked problems either.
- Every wicked problem can be considered a symptom of another problem.
- There is no single way to explain the nature of a wicked problem: numerous possible explanations exist. As a consequence, the 'chosen' explanation defines the direction of the resolution.

When we focus on poverty, for example, we can have a look at the nine characteristics of a wicked problem described above. First, it is hard – or impossible – to give an exact formulation of the problem of poverty. What exactly is poverty? The term poverty obviously applies to people who lack basic human needs. But how do we define poverty as a social problem? Is it the number of people in a country who have less than a certain amount of money? If so, have we formulated the problem well enough? Should we include underlying factors and their interplay? Should we look at food access, housing, and health, or also include other factors like education? When trying to solve the problem, what exactly defines 'success'? When is the problem solved? When implementing policies to eradicate poverty, we can define whether the policies are having a positive or a negative effect. But when they appear to worsen the problem, we cannot undo their implementation (there is no trial and error). Furthermore, poverty can be caused by problems such as political instability, social injustice, unemployment, oppression, overpopulation, among many other possible causes, all of which are wicked problems in themselves.

Today, academic research is expected to provide a basis for policies and interventions that contribute to solving societal problems. As indicated above, most of these societal problems derive from complex interactions. Therefore, addressing them typically requires an interdisciplinary or transdisciplinary approach.

Driver 4: Generative technologies

Generative technologies have been identified as a fourth driver of interdisciplinary research (NAS 2005). Generative technologies are technologies that allow for new applications of great value and are capable of transforming existing disciplines and generating new fields, as the NAS put it. Generative technologies are able to give birth to new possibilities, and thereby widen the scope of (interdisciplinary) research. Furthermore, generative technologies, such as magnetic resonance imaging (MRI), sometimes prompt collaborations between academics from different disciplines that would not have happened otherwise.

An example of the widening scope of interdisciplinary research as a consequence of technologies is the recent revolution in data collection and data mining, and the increased computational power allows scientists to analyze complex systems in radically new ways. Computer models allow scientists to understand the underlying forces, interactions, and non-linearities that together constitute complex phenomena (van Santen, Khoe & Vermeer 2010). Another example is the study of the human brain, which dates back thousands of years but it is only recently that scientists have begun to try and map the human brain and its cognitive processes. These generative technologies have allowed for the development of new theories such as the neural network theory, have given us greater insight into various clinical conditions (e.g. hemiplegia, the one-sided paralysis of the body), and have created new fields such as computational neurobiology.

6 Interdisciplinary integration

When we distinguished between multidisciplinarity and interdisciplinarity in chapter 4, we pointed out that the synthesis or integration of disciplinary insights is the defining characteristic of interdisciplinarity. Subsequently, we gave an overview of possible drivers of interdisciplinary research in chapter 5. Once groups of scientists from different disciplines or fields bring their respective disciplinary expertise to the table, the question arises how to integrate these with each other. This is not an easy task, as different disciplinary academics tend to think and do research in different ways as a consequence of their different disciplinary educations.

So let us now zoom in on interdisciplinary integration itself. What exactly does integration mean? And how can insights from different academic disciplines be integrated, especially when they appear to be incommensurate or in conflict with each other? In this chapter, we will introduce the process of interdisciplinary integration, and how and when it is done. Moreover, we will provide a set of different approaches to integration. In box 3 we give an example (ADHD in school-aged children) that illustrates the added value of an integrated interdisciplinary approach.

Box 3
ADHD in school-aged children

Attention deficit hyperactive disorder (ADHD) is a mental disorder and, at the same time, a societal problem of significant proportions. In the US, for example, between two and four million school-aged children are affected by the disorder, showing symptoms such as hyperactivity, lack of concentration, and impulsivity. However, a thorough understanding of ADHD has not yet been arrived at. This drove Lauren Dean, a student at Miami University, to conduct an interdisciplinary study to unravel what is preventing us from understanding the causes of ADHD (Newell, 2006). To start, Dean mapped out the different assumptions and views on ADHD from the different disciplines that provide insights into the problem. She found that scientists from the fields of biology, psychology, and medicine tend to categorize ADHD as a biological disorder that needs biological intervention in the form of medication, although they realize that it cannot be diagnosed by physical tests alone, like other disorders of biological origin. Academics with a background in sociology, social history, or culture

▼

studies, in contrast, think the causes of ADHD are social and cultural, and often reject a physiological explanation of ADHD. Scholars from the field of educational science agree with the first group that ADHD is a medical problem, but also converge with the social causes of ADHD, as some hypothesize that parenting behavior is the main cause of the onset of ADHD, rather than biological factors. In other words, Dean found that the different disciplinary explanations of ADHD are a perfect example of the nature-nurture debate: the debate on whether something is caused by genes (nature) or by the social environment (nurture).

Moreover, Dean found that the concept of childhood had changed over the last couple of centuries and that it is primarily a socially and culturally constructed concept. As a consequence of the increase in employment of women during the last half century, the concept of childhood has undergone changes, as children are placed in kindergartens and pre-schools. Therefore, the definitions of 'normal' and 'deviant' behavior of children have also shifted accordingly. In these educational spaces, behavior now classified as typical of ADHD has become increasingly problematic. Subsequently, children who do not fit the ideals of their parents and do not concur with contemporary educational ideology are increasingly labeled ADHD.

The main problem, Dean states, is that the disciplines concerned with ADHD use different definitions of ADHD-type behavior and often employ different definitions for the terms 'normal', 'deviant', and 'childhood'. As a consequence, a comprehensive understanding of ADHD is still lacking. Through interdisciplinary integration and by redefining key concepts, one can move toward a better understanding of this disorder.

The example above illustrates the need for and value of interdisciplinary integration. But what is meant by integration? Interdisciplinary integration can be defined as the synthesis of two or more disciplinary insights – drawn from different perspectives – into new knowledge. An important step in integration is to identify which disciplines are necessary for a complete understanding of the problem. Then, one has to uncover which assumptions underlie each discipline. More generally, what are the disciplines' paradigms? Disciplinary academics are largely unaware of some of their assumptions, and interdisciplinary dialogue helps to reveal those assumptions. Note that in today's research practice, interdisciplinary integration often occurs but is rarely described. As researchers are asked to report on the results of their interdisciplinary endeavor – and not so much the process that has led them to integrate the different findings – they are usually not focused on this process. Although integration is common practice at DRIFT, Loorbach, for example, has trouble stating when exactly it happens: "It is hard to pinpoint when and where interdisciplinary integration happens, since it's a normal condition for us. I don't recognize when it happens exactly; I'd only recognize it if it didn't happen. And that never happens in practice, because it's the core of our work."

Although it is usually not described, interdisciplinary integration often forms the basis for a new and more comprehensive understanding of the problem being studied. Integration is primarily a cognitive process enabling scientists to combine different (disciplinary) concepts, methodologies, or theories that, at first glance, have no readily apparent connection or commonality.

6.1   Communication as a first step to integration

Interdisciplinary integration begins with communication across disciplinary boundaries, revealing differences but also highlighting similarities between the insights derived from different disciplines. This can be a challenge. There are plentiful examples of scientists who argue against each other (often from within the safe borders of their own discipline) instead of creating a productive dialogue. This is often the result of their making various implicit assumptions pertaining to their respective disciplines. Inexplicit misunderstandings may then arise concerning what is deemed a valuable question, what are valid data, what kind of result (publication, intervention, technology) should emerge from the research project, and so on. Clearly, as scientists are often unaware of the implicit assumptions of their discipline, such assumptions will only become explicit when they engage with each other in an open and extended dialogue with each other based upon mutual trust and respect.

An open mind and the courage to step outside of one's comfort zone are essential characteristics for a productive dialogue. Jeroen van Dongen, professor of History of Science at Utrecht University and the University of Amsterdam (pers. comm., 4 December 2013): "When you study, you submerge yourself in the culture of that discipline. You learn not only its knowledge, but also its cultural values and norms. In interdisciplinary research, talking with someone from another discipline means you are meeting someone from another culture. When doing so, you have to 'a-culturalize' from your disciplinary backgrounds." Julie Thompson-Klein (1996) even contends that interdisciplinarians, as members of a new social and cognitive community, form a new, shared language, a creole. When you study a topic that falls within a specific interdisciplinary field, you have to learn the creole of that field as well.

In the example of ADHD, psychologists, sociologists, and biologists had to overcome several challenges in order to come to a fruitful dialogue. Psychologists and biologists tend to categorize ADHD as a biological disorder, whereas academics from the fields of sociology and cultural studies think the causes of ADHD are social and cultural. In addition to these differences, both views also have similarities – they share 'common ground' – as biologists, for example, realize that the disorder is diagnosed in a social context and psychologists are aware of the biological processes underlying a patient's behavior and cognition. In order to overcome the differences arising from the different disciplines, certain components (that are relevant to the research problem) of the participating disciplines need to be modified. As you can see in the example of ADHD, the different disciplinary definitions of 'normal', 'deviant' and 'childhood' needed adjustment. Such modification of components can be accomplished in various ways and on various levels (corresponding with different research phases), as is explained below.

There have been specific questionnaires and dialogue techniques developed in order to guide interdisciplinary team communication and collaboration (see the list with further readings and websites for some references). Once the differences and similarities between disciplinary contributions are examined, one can move on to the next challenge: creating common ground. By this we mean reinterpreting these differences in order to bring out commonalities between the disciplines. This forms the preparation for interdisciplinary integration.

6.2   Integration techniques

Recalling our discussion in chapter 2 of the Science Cycle and the main ingredients that determine what science is: starting with pre-existing theories and laws a scientist engages in the reasoning processes deduction and induction and comes up with new predictions and conjectures. These are then operationalized and investigated by turning toward the world or reality. After the process of data collection and observation of facts, the scientist might think that inductive reasoning toward an adjusted or new theory is warranted. During all of this, the scientist would best articulate relevant implicit assumptions and acknowledge the theoretical and methodological pluralism involved. We will observe that several of these ingredients and phases in the Science Cycle turn out to be important for the process of interdisciplinary integration.

As touched upon above, integration may take place in different ways and at different levels. Newell (2006) introduced a set of integrative techniques to carry out trans- and interdisciplinary integration. We categorize this concrete set of techniques into three broader classes of integration methods. First, one can add one or more elements from another discipline to a certain disciplinary theory, method, or result. Second, disciplinary theories, methods, or results can be adjusted using insights from other disciplines and, third, in some cases it is possible to connect several disciplines around a central idea. Note that in practice a combination of these techniques is not uncommon. We present them here separately, but in practice – as you will experience while engaging in interdisciplinary research yourself – they form a continuum, as integration usually takes place at multiple stages of the research process (illustrated in figure 7).

Add

One can add an element from another discipline to a disciplinary theory, for example by using the technique of extension. Differences or oppositions in disciplinary concepts can sometimes be addressed when one extends the meaning of an idea beyond the domain of the discipline into the domain of another discipline. Robert Frank (as reported in Newell, 2007), for instance, extended the meaning of 'self-interest' in economics from its short-term context. He included the long term, because, as he argued, someone who acts out of self-interest in the short term may create a reputation that is not beneficial to self-interest in the long term. In other words, he extended the economic meaning of self-interest with insights from sociology and evolutionary biology. As a result, the scope of his theory of self-interest was much larger than that of previous economic theories and so was the domain in which the theory was applicable.

Adjust

When commonalities in concepts or assumptions are obscured by discipline-specific terminology, you can adjust the concept by giving it a new name and a meaning that does justice to your interdisciplinary insight. In other words, you will create a new term that captures the commonality in the current terms.

To adjust a concept, one can use the technique of redefinition. An example is the research by Janet Delph, as described by Repko (2007). She identified three disciplines that are most relevant for crime investigation: criminal investigation (justice), forensic science (biology, chemistry), and forensic psychology. A source of differences or conflict between these sub-disciplines is their preference for two different investigatory methods and reliance on two kinds of evidence: physical evidence (forensic science), and intuition born of extensive experience and insights from crime scene analysis (forensic psychology). By redefining these methods together as 'profiling', Delph was able to bridge the natural sciences (i.e. forensic science) and the behavioral sciences (i.e. forensic psychology and criminal investigation). She was then able to demonstrate how specialists from the fields of criminal investigation, forensic science, and forensic psychology could integrate their knowledge. This implies that when no adequate traces are available to forensic scientists for analysis, 'profiling' can still move on by, for example, using a combination of 'intuition' born of extensive experience and insights derived from crime scene analysis.

When concepts or assumptions appear to be diametrically opposed, the technique of transformation can be used. For example, economists traditionally define humans as rational agents, whereas most sociologists hold humans as irrational. This difference, or conflict, between disciplinary perspectives can be resolved by changing a dichotomous assumption about rationality into a continuous variable. As a result, the notion of (ir)rationality becomes a variable instead of an assumption; instead of either/or, we are now able to determine different degrees of rationality in humans, partly influenced by their social conditions – as was shown with the example on poverty above.

Connect

When key concepts have the same name but different meanings in different disciplines, it is helpful to draw a concept map and define and connect the different meanings of the particular concept. The technique of organization can help to capture the different conceptualizations of the term and thus integrate them in a global interdisciplinary way. Newell (2007), for example, describes how Boulding recognized that both benevolent behavior (studied by sociologists) and malevolent behavior (studied by political scientists) can be understood as other-regarding behavior (studied by political scientists). He connected the concepts by placing them along a continuum of other-regarding behavior, with the self-interested behavior studied by economists as the midpoint, because its degree of other-regarding behavior is zero. Boulding used the technique of organization to integrate differing conceptions of human nature underlying economics, sociology, and political science, and transformed the debate about whether human nature in general is selfish or altruistic into a choice of where on the continuum of motivations people are likely to fall in the particular complex problem under study.

In many cases, integration relies upon a mixture of the three categories of integration techniques and has implication for theories, methods as well as results. Environmental sciences and other sustainability related studies, for example, often employ optimization functions in order to determine a solution for a particular problem that is sustainable both in economic, social, and ecological terms and not just in either one of these. Adding and connecting theoretical insights into the relevant variables will help to develop the complex optimization function necessary for such calculations. When scientists use these optimization functions they may also use the figures or graphs result from them, providing an additional and visual mode of presentation that can be helpful for a team discussion.

Other options for integration

Obviously, these three categories are not exhausting all options for integration of insights. Another and long-standing technique for combining insights from two or more disciplines into a problem, is reasoning by analogy or metaphor. Some cognitive scientists, for example, describe thinking as a form of computing. Consequently, they can use some principles of digital computing to formulate hypotheses on thought processes or employ other insights or methods from computational science in their study of human cognition.

Apart from distinguishing between techniques of integration, we can also distinguish between different levels at which such integration can take place. Newell (pers. comm., 3 December 2013), for example, states that integration can take place at the level of concepts, theories, and methods. All these levels involve parts of disciplinary paradigms, and when creating common ground between them, one can subsequently truly integrate and form new, interdisciplinary insights. However, we would argue that in broad interdisciplinary research projects, integration may also take place at the level of results, as illustrated by the example of a research project on sustainable energy on p. 98, in which disciplines as unrelated as political science and physics come together. The three levels (or research phases) are included in figure 7: theory (which here includes concepts), methods, and results.

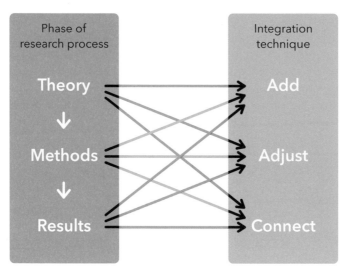

Figure 7   *Overview of integration techniques*

These different strategies to achieve integration are further examined in part 2, but first let us try to clarify these strategies by means of the example on sustainable fisheries in box 4.

Box 4
Sustainable fisheries

Managing fisheries was traditionally a matter of landing as many fish as possible. The focus was on controlling the amount of fish, in order to secure, or even increase, profit margins. This mode of management can be classified as management-as-control, and its resources (e.g. fish) were considered commodities. Moreover, the ecosystem and the social system were viewed as completely separate (Berkes, 2003).

This approach inevitably led to the overexploitation of fish stocks, causing collapses in fish populations all over the world. Different stakeholders started to clash when conflicts between ecological, economic, social, and cultural interests emerged (Charles, 1994). Thus, the need arose for a renewed and integrated approach to fishery management. In response, a new approach to fishery management was developed, in which certain key elements were redefined. There were no longer two separate systems (fish ecosystem and human social system), but one integrated socio-ecological system.

The type of integration occurring here can be described as connecting theories (in this case from the fields of ecology and social sciences). Moreover, fish stocks were redefined as ecosystem components with their own niches and functions instead of simply as a commodity. In effect, a concept (which is a component of a theory) was adjusted. Lastly, the management-as-control approach was replaced by an approach focusing on managing for resilience (Berkes, 2003), thus constituting an adjustment of a method. As a result, fisheries have become more sustainable and the social benefits linked to them have become more stable.

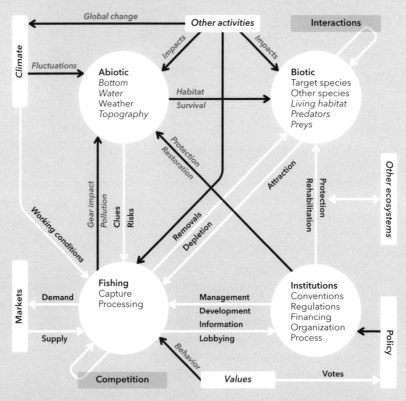

Figure 8   An integrated model of the socio-ecological system around fisheries
(Garcia & Cochrane, 2005). Reprinted with permission from the publisher

Thus, many problems that require an interdisciplinary research approach encompass a range of interrelated systems/subsystems, mechanisms, and/or processes. Interdisciplinary research on these problems involves analyzing how these different components are related to each other. A conceptual model can therefore be a valuable tool. In figure 8, a conceptual model of the socio-ecological system of fisheries is displayed. As you can see, the various subsystems are the different research areas of disciplines ranging from ecology, climatology, and earth sciences, to economics, political science, and jurisprudence. Their theories are connected and this visualization makes clear how they are related and influence each other.

The above example of sustainable fisheries also shows that integration of scientific insights can be carried out with other means than by focusing on science ingredients like theories, concepts, laws, and the like. Indeed, visual means can often be very useful in facilitating and specifying such integration, as graphs, tables, and schemas often involve a specific alignment of different features of a particular phenomenon, which then invites further reasoning about the apparent structure of this alignment. A famous example is the 'hockey-stick curve' published in 1999 by climate scientists Mann, Bradley, and Hughes in which temperature variations over time since the year 1000 are shown, indicating a strong increase in rising temperatures since the nineteenth century. Further alignment of this figure with data about industrialization subsequently suggested that it may be useful to investigate an explanatory mechanism that would allow integration of these data. A still different mode of integrating insights occurs when engineers develop constructions that are both in accordance with scientific insights and with ergonomic requirements or when a social policy is developed that takes into account the cultural norms of a specific target group. In other words, developing an interdisciplinary (or transdisciplinary) integration of insights not only requires knowledge in pertinent insights but can often also depend upon an interdisciplinary team's creative imagination.

You have now completed the first part and have gained an initial understanding of interdisciplinarity. You have learned what science is, how academia is organized into different disciplines and what these disciplines can accomplish. You have also learned that the complex nature of many problems demands an interdisciplinary research approach. And finally, you have learned that integration is a key aspect of interdisciplinary research.

In part 2, we will present a model on how to perform interdisciplinary research. We will guide you through the interdisciplinary research process step by step. We will give you tips, teach you tricks, and show you examples of interdisciplinary research projects that we believe will provide a solid basis for your own interdisciplinary research project.

Part 2
The Manual
'The How'

In this part, we will guide you through the interdisciplinary research process. We begin by pointing out the different phases of this process, then describe it in its entirety and indicate which parts are of particular interest for interdisciplinary researchers. In short, we guide you through the problem and the research question, the theoretical framework, the methods and techniques of research, data collection and analysis, and finally, the discussion and conclusion. As integration is a defining characteristic of interdisciplinary research, different integration techniques that were briefly introduced in chapter 5 will be illustrated with examples of previous student research projects.

The steps you need to take to complete an interdisciplinary research project might overwhelm you. As an undergraduate, for example, you might not feel comfortable dissecting the theoretical background of your own discipline. But do not be discouraged: you will find that after going through the process a couple of times, you will increasingly feel at ease being an interdisciplinary researcher. All beginnings are hard, to some degree. But when you have the right mindset and attitude, you will succeed!

7 The interdisciplinary research process

Although there are a lot of similarities between the disciplinary research process (with which you might already be familiar) and the interdisciplinary research process, there are some additional questions to answer, steps to perform, and challenges to overcome with regard toin the latter. We have therefore developed a model for doing interdisciplinary research (see box 5 and figure 9). Building on this model, we describe the different stages of the research process and the additional challenges interdisciplinary researchers are facing.

In part 1, we mentioned several drivers of interdisciplinary research, among which the inherent complexity of nature and society and the need to solve societal problems. However, in a student project you might not be pressured by such a driver to conduct interdisciplinary research, as the starting point may be different from academic research in practice. In some cases, students form a research team on the basis of their different educational backgrounds, and then collectively formulate a subject or a problem to investigate. Although the drivers described in part 1 might cover the problem or subject, the main driver in choosing a subject is usually the student's personal experience and practice.

7.1 The IIS model of interdisciplinary research

In figure 9 we present our model for interdisciplinary research. It describes a generalized research process, in which the following steps are distinguished: identify the problem or topic (i) and formulate the preliminary research question (ii) in the Orientation phase; develop the theoretical framework (iii), finalize the research question (iv) and sub-questions (vi) and research methods and design (vii) in the Preparation phase; collect and analyze the data (viii) in the Data phase; and interpret the results, draw conclusions and write the discussion (ix) in the Finalization phase. As convenient as this may seem, it is important to note that there is not really a standard research process, not only because research processes differ in practice, but also because what is considered a normal research process differs from discipline to discipline. Therefore, the model that is proposed here should serve as a guideline during your own research, not as a strict protocol.

In chapter 12, you will find an example of a complete interdisciplinary research project as carried out by students who used our model as a guideline. The example focuses on an innovative and sustainable form of greenhouse agriculture called Fogponics. It will help you to get an idea of how our research model can be operationalized.

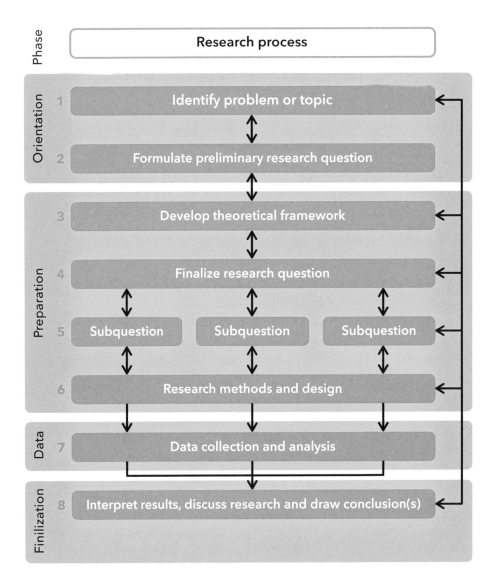

Figure 9   The IIS model for interdisciplinary research

In this model for the interdisciplinary research process, we use different steps (blue boxes in the middle of the figure) reflecting the tasks you must complete in a specific phase of your research (indicated in the left margin). Although you may sometimes need to return to a previous step, the order of steps is more or less fixed and you should not skip a single one. As an obvious example, you cannot analyze data that you have not yet collected. However, it is important to realize that you need to think one step ahead (i.e. you need to know how you are going to analyze your data before you start collecting them). For this reason, we have grouped together several steps in the following phases of the interdisciplinary research process: Orientation, Preparation, Data collection and analysis, and Finalization.

Phase 1   Orientation

You might start your research process by choosing a topic that fits your interests, or a problem that you would like to solve. In all cases, you need to explore the topic, find out which disciplines have something relevant to say about it, and then decide whether an interdisciplinary approach is justified at all. In short, you have to go through an orientation phase. A challenge for interdisciplinary research is ensuring each relevant discipline is reflected in the choice and wording of the research topic and that at this early point of the project no single discipline is dominant. Furthermore, you have to formulate a preliminary research question to define the focus of your research (see chapter 8). This forms the basis to create a theoretical framework (see chapter 9), which you will develop in the next phase.

Phase 2   Preparation

Preparing a scientific research requires the development of a theoretical framework, usually drawn from a literature search: scientists build upon the work of predecessors and colleagues, as was mentioned in chapter 2. The theoretical framework that must be developed is the result of a thorough literature research, gives an overview of the 'state of the art' (the most relevant theories and data on the research topic), and provides a systemized analysis of the most important findings. In the case of interdisciplinary research, this overview will consist of publications from different disciplines.

While analyzing the different disciplinary parts of the theoretical framework, you need to be constantly aware of the different disciplinary points of view (see figures 1 and 2 in chapter 1) with regard to the topic. This awareness of the differences between disciplinary perspectives will enable you to seek or create common ground (as will be explained in detail in chapter 10) at a later stage. As we have seen in part 1, finding common ground forms the basis for the integration of (some of) the different disciplinary insights into the problem. The integration of such insights will enable you to ask an insightful integrated interdisciplinary research question (step 4, explained in chapter 9).

After you have identified the common ground between the disciplines involved, it is time to think of the best way to answer your research question. What are the sub-questions arising from your main research question and which disciplines can address these questions? Please note that sub-questions can be both interdisciplinary and monodisciplinary.

In addition, you should also consider which methods and techniques are most suitable to answer the subquestions (see chapter 10). As mentioned in part 1, it is important to note that the chosen method(s) and technique(s) partly determine the kinds of results you will obtain. In certain cases, it will be useful to integrate multiple disciplinary research methods and techniques in order to get to a more complete answer to your questions (see chapter 10).

When you have (i) identified the problem; (ii) formulated a preliminary research question; (iii) developed an integrated theoretical framework; (iv) finalized the research question; and (v) designed a research outline (developed a methodology) to answer the research question, you will have completed the theoretical stage of your research. You should now have the information necessary to write a research proposal or literature study.

It may appear strange that conceiving a research proposal consumes so much time and attention. However, on second thought the reason for this should be obvious. As you can imagine, writing a research proposal is a crucial part of your research, as you need to formulate and plan the entire project before you begin collecting data. So, the more effort you put into writing a well-thought-out and integrated interdisciplinary research proposal, the more likely it is that your interdisciplinary research project will be a success.

Remember that by doing interdisciplinary research, you will be entering a field that is possibly completely new to you and perhaps even to your supervisor. As you will be connecting disciplines and fields, you will most likely be unable to rely on your prior disciplinary experience to guide you. You will therefore need to set out a detailed, clear-cut process to guide you as you try to engage in the holistic thinking required for interdisciplinary integration. The model for interdisciplinary research will serve as a general guideline, but you need to map out in detail how you will apply its guidelines to your specific project, and you have to do so in advance so that you will not flounder in the morass of (sometimes conflicting) disciplinary details in which you will soon find yourself (W.H. Newell, pers. comm., 3 December 2013). It is important to keep in mind that along the road you may discover several other disciplinary insights that somehow touch upon your problem. However, in the preparation phase you have investigated what the most relevant disciplinary contributions to answering your research question are and therefore you should not always feel tempted to include those later discoveries.

Phase 3   Data collection and analysis

After your research proposal has been completed and accepted, you can begin the practical stage of your research and start collecting data – of whatever nature they may be. This phase starts off with the operationalization of your main questions and sub-questions into research methods in order to obtain data. Once you have collected the data needed to answer your questions, you have to think about ways to analyze the data (see chapter 11).

Phase 4   Finalization

Although some research projects might invite an implementation of the results, we will here stick to the research process itself. As presenting research results always entails a consideration of its limitations and future extensions or follow-ups, we will finish the process by providing a discussion and conclusion. Formulating a discussion and conclusion in interdisciplinary research might be more difficult than in monodisciplinary research. You have to integrate the results and insights related to your sub-questions and you also have to ensure that you actually answer your research question and reflect on your answer by referring to your integrated theoretical framework. The differences and overlap you have found between different disciplinary insights in the theoretical stage of your research will help you to understand the implications of your results and will give more insight into the topic.

It is important to note that the research process is an iterative process, a process in which a cycle of operations is usually executed more than once, gradually bringing one closer to some optimal condition or goal. You will start with a topic or question and finish with a conclusion, but in between you will most probably need to go back and forth between the different phases of the research process. This 'movement' is likely to affect your research question, which you may need to rephrase during different stages of the research. Conversely, if you have made changes to your theoretical framework, your discussion and conclusion will not remain the same as these will refer to that framework. Especially in the preparation phase, iteration is likely to be important. As you collect more information, this will continuously influence your research question.

7.2 Planning your research project

As you can imagine, an interdisciplinary research project is a major assignment that requires even more planning than 'normal' research, especially when you are working in a team. A lot of time has to be invested in the coordination of the different subprojects and communication between the contributing researchers. More than in monodisciplinary research, interdisciplinary research demands openness and flexibility of the academic as well as collegiality when you are working as a team. As you can imagine, the different (disciplinary) sub-projects are likely to be executed at different moments of time, as – for example – the results of one sub-project might form the starting point of a second sub-project. Therefore, it is highly important to think about a sound planning when you are about to begin an interdisciplinary research project. Of course, some parts of the project can turn out to be more time consuming than expected. It is particularly important to realize that composing and writing your final research report can take a considerable amount of time. Thus, try to make a flexible planning to be able to cope with such unexpected surprises, and try to leave some time at the end of the project open to be able to finish the final report in a good way. The time schedule for a six-month bachelor-level research project is likely to resemble the one displayed in figure 10.

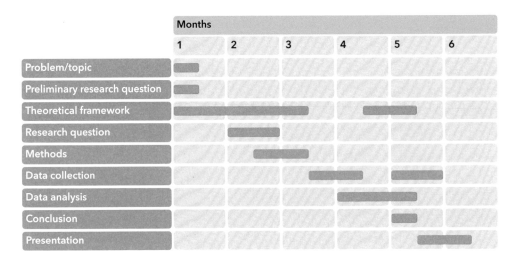

Figure 10   Time schedule for a bachelor research project

8 The problem

After the first preview of the IIS model of interdisciplinary research, we will now zoom in on the different phases and guide you through the steps of the model in more detail. In any research project, the first task at hand is to narrow down the problem or topic to a research question that can be answered in the time available. Especially in interdisciplinary research this can be a challenging step as it always involves a complex problem (see chapter 5), which can (and should be) be studied from multiple perspectives or disciplines. Here, we will describe the first two steps of our interdisciplinary research model (figure 11). How to narrow down a complex problem to a preliminary research question that is feasible in both time and scale is the central topic of this chapter.

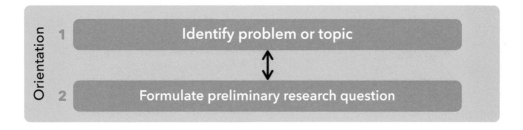

Figure 11   Steps 1 and 2 of the IIS model for interdisciplinary research

Considerations:
- Consider all relevant disciplines: which 3 to 4 disciplines are most relevant?
- What are the dominant perspectives of those disciplines on the problem or area of interest?

Step 1   Identify problem or topic

Finding a topic is not always easy. An additional challenge in the case of student projects is to find a problem that can be addressed by the available disciplinary expertise in the research team (see box 5 for an exercise that you can use when trying to find a shared topic of interest). But it is equally important to find something that triggers your academic curiosity.

Box 5

Brainstorm exercise: Finding a shared topic of interest via 'triangulation'

If an interdisciplinary team consists of a given combination of disciplines it may be somewhat challenging to develop a shared topic as usually scientists start with a topic and then assemble the necessary team. However, determining the 'overlap' between several disciplines can be done by performing a 'triangulation' exercise. The term triangulation refers to the process that, for example, allows mobile phone providers to precisely determine the position of your mobile phone at the intersection of three or more antennas' areas.

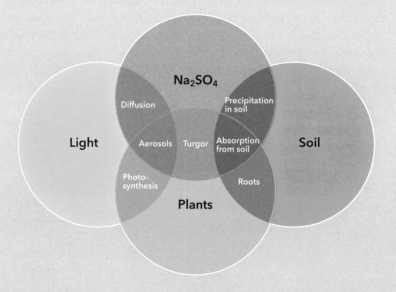

An example of triangulation: combining insights from chemistry, geography, plant physiology and physics, a group of students has decided to investigate the impact of sodium sulphate from volcanic eruptions on the environment and particularly in plants (Gelauff, Gravemaker, Isarin & Waajen, 2015).

You might similarly determine a specific and shared topic by together following these steps:

▼

1 Write down individually and from your disciplinary perspective a list of topics that interest you, taking into account what might be of interest to other disciplines.
2 Exchange the different lists of topics with each other and look for one or more topics that show similarity or overlap with others.
3 Consider individually what sub-questions arising from such topics your discipline could answer and formulate a preliminary research question.
4 Again, discuss in the team the different topics and the sets of sub-questions related to those topics that each member has formulated, choosing the most relevant or fruitful topic for further elaboration.

Sometimes a brainstorm session can lead to the discovery of a knowledge gap that can be addressed with an interdisciplinary research question. A student who was educated in both law and interdisciplinary social sciences found an interesting discrepancy between the two fields. In literature from the fields of political science and sociology, he found explanations for the fact that in the Netherlands in recent years there had been an increase in the societal call for stricter penalties for criminal acts. Theories from the field of law, on the other hand, provided convincing arguments against strong punishments.

The question why the societal call for stricter penalties continues to exist, despite the strong arguments from judges that stronger punishment does not work had not yet been asked, and thus not answered. It provided the basis for an interdisciplinary research project on the effects of societal and political criticism on the judiciary in the Netherlands (Noyon, 2012).

Once you have decided on a topic or a problem that you want to focus on in your project, you need to set a starting point for your research. The answers to the following questions can be a good starting point for your initial literature research, and they can help to clarify the context of your topic of research.
1 What do I already know about the problem?
2 What aspects, related to the problem, are important to consider?
3 What other problems does it relate to?
4 From which perspectives can I look at this problem?

It can be very helpful to visualize your answers to these questions in a concept map or a similar illustration. For example, the mind map below (figure 12) was built around the topic of disaster risk reduction. Drawing a mind map in which you visualize as many relevant aspects pertaining to the topic as possible can help you to decide on a preliminary research question (Step 2 of the research model).

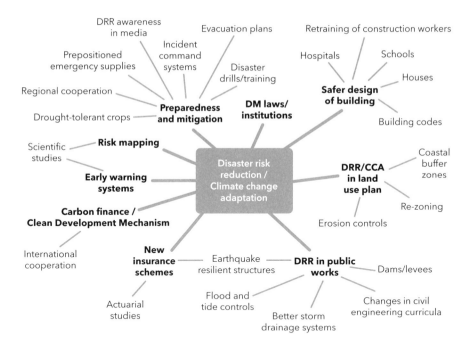

Figure 12   Example of a mind map (Talisayon, 2010). Reprinted with permission from the author

Another way to reveal the most relevant aspects pertaining to the research topic is the development of a mechanistic model, which is commonly used in the life sciences and the cognitive sciences and is gradually being adopted in the social sciences as well. Discussing it here may also help you to realize how the different steps in the interdisciplinary research process are connected with each other, because a mechanistic model can be useful both when you are developing your research question and when attempting to integrate new results from your interdisciplinary research. Take, for example, the mechanistic or mechanism-based explanation of action understanding, which helps to explain how humans are capable of understanding other people's actions at several levels of complexity. Interdisciplinary research by cognitive neuroscientists, hermeneutic scholars, and others can clarify the complex cognitive mechanisms that develop over time, enabling humans to understand actions that consist not just of bodily behavior but of verbally expressed intentions and narratives as well (Keestra, 2012). Let us pause for a moment to see how this works and how such an approach can be useful at several phases of the interdisciplinary research process.

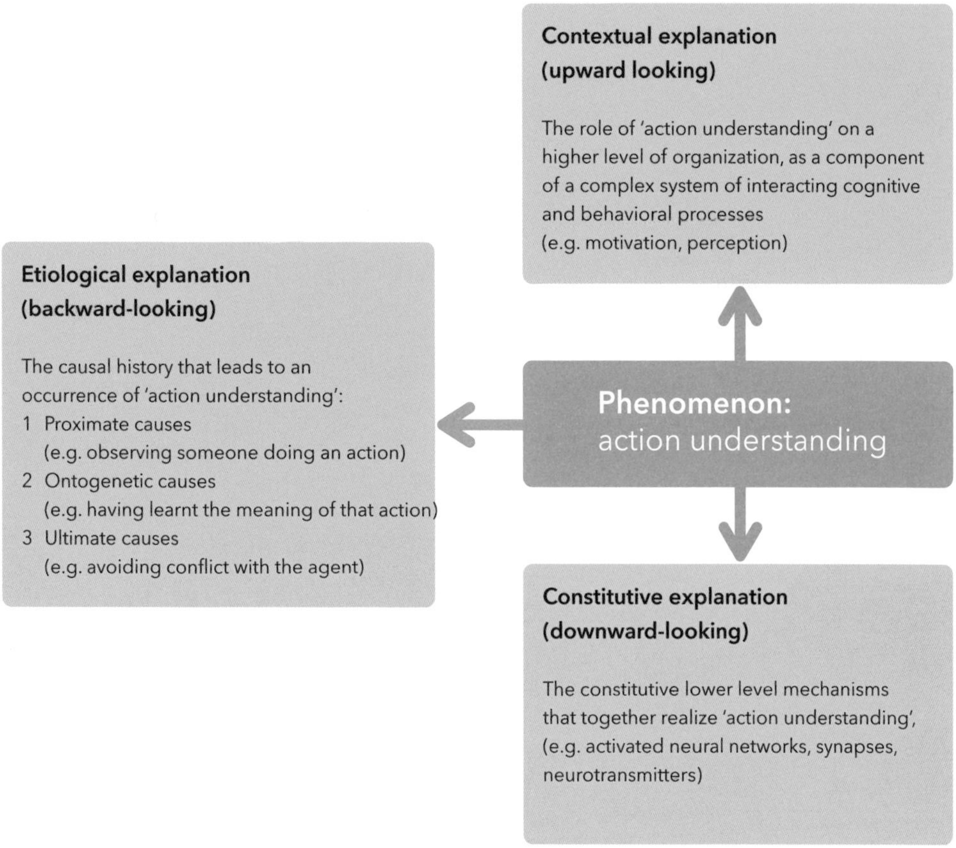

**Contextual explanation
(upward looking)**

The role of 'action understanding' on a
higher level of organization, as a component
of a complex system of interacting cognitive
and behavioral processes
(e.g. motivation, perception)

**Etiological explanation
(backward-looking)**

The causal history that leads to an
occurrence of 'action understanding':
1 Proximate causes
  (e.g. observing someone doing an action)
2 Ontogenetic causes
  (e.g. having learnt the meaning of that action)
3 Ultimate causes
  (e.g. avoiding conflict with the agent)

**Phenomenon:
action understanding**

**Constitutive explanation
(downward-looking)**

The constitutive lower level mechanisms
that together realize 'action understanding',
(e.g. activated neural networks, synapses,
neurotransmitters)

*Figure 13   Different explanations of a phenomenon, for example the phenomenon 'action
understanding' by a human subject (adapted from Valli, 2011)*

Figure 13 shows how scientists can develop and integrate different types of
explanation in order to reach a more comprehensive explanation of a particular
phenomenon, like a case of action understanding, or the decrease of fish stocks
in the North Sea, or the financial crisis in the EU. The figure suggests that we can
approach such a phenomenon from various perspectives that together might offer a
more comprehensive explanation. Obviously, a complex phenomenon is constituted
by component mechanisms, such as when many activated neural networks together
constitute action understanding, or when the financial situation is determined
by markets, institutions, selling and buying behaviors, and so on. Similarly, the
phenomenon (as much as its component mechanisms, like the ones just mentioned)
can be partly explained by looking into its history, in which both short- and
long-term processes play distinctive roles. In addition, one could also consider
how the phenomenon itself responds to its context: the phenomenon of action
understanding is also interacting with other cognitive and behavioral processes, fish
stock is responsive to a wider eco-system and the EU participates in global financial
networks.

What may become apparent to you from looking at figure 13 is that when you are collaborating with scientists from different perspectives you might still contribute to explaining the same phenomenon. Yet it also suggests that it takes an additional effort to ensure that your investigations are coordinated with each other; otherwise it can happen, for example, that the etiological explanation offered by a developmental scientist might be only indirectly related to the genetic explanation developed by a colleague and not even touch upon the sociological explanation suggested by yet another colleague. It would be better if you search for a research topic that facilitates such coordinated research together, such as when the cognitive process investigated by the developmental scientist is probably determined by genes that are available for genetic screening and is also involved in a form of social interaction. Discussing a phenomenon's comprehensive explanation, possibly with the help of a visual representation, might be helpful in this process.

The result of such collaborations is that the insights into a phenomenon – in the form of mechanistic explanation or otherwise – will, over time become more and more elaborated. A good example of an increasingly detailed and specified mechanistic explanation is the climate model that is developed by the IPCC (Le Treut, Somerville, Cubasch, Ding, Mauritzen et al., 2007). Through the years, climate scientists discovered additional components that are part of the mechanism that constitute our climate system. The evolution of the model of the explanatory mechanism from the 1970s onwards is illustrated in Figure 14.

This again suggests how such a model can be useful at various stages of research. Obviously, a mechanistic model is valuable as it can be employed as an integration technique for your results and theory (for other practical tips on how to come to an integrated research question, see chapter 10). However, in the context of identifying a problem or topic, a closer look at such a model might also be fruitful. For example, by scrutinizing the models, one might develop predictions or hypotheses about the involvement of oceans not only in absorbing sulphates and other substances, but also in absorbing and reflecting sunlight radiation. Indeed, it can be very useful for an interdisciplinary team to start its research by discussing one or more of such models.

The World in Global Climate Models

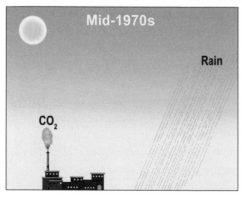
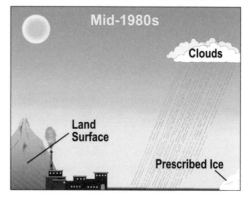
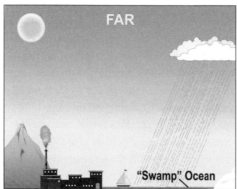
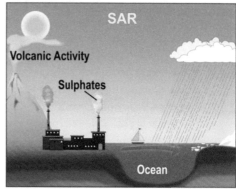
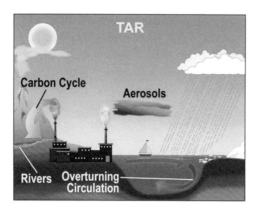
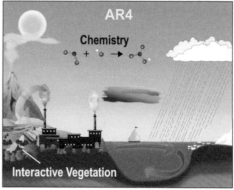

Figure 14   The evolution of climate change models as developed by the IPCC (Le Treut, Somerville, Cubasch., Ding, Mauritzen et al., 2007). Reprinted with permission from the author.

Once you have identified the problem or topic, you need to know from which perspectives the problem can be addressed. A first important consideration here is to identify the disciplines that are most relevant to the problem or topic. When you consider all relevant theories and methods, which 3 or 4 disciplines are most important for researching the problem? Subsequently, you can flesh out these perspectives: what are those disciplines' dominant perspectives on the problem or area of interest?

How do you select the most important disciplines for your problem? A good starting point would be the overview of disciplines and their main topics put together by Szostak [and presented in Repko (2012)]. Another way is to go through the content pages and introduction of introductory textbooks, pertinent encyclopedias, and compendiums that cover a field, relevant conference proceedings, or other comprehensive volumes. Such carefully edited volumes offer overviews that are very hard to get from browsing on the internet or in digital libraries. While going through the content pages and the introduction, you will usually be able to identify the phenomena studied, the main assumptions, and the more general theories of the field. This can provide a good starting point from which to gain an understanding of the different perspectives and assumptions that different fields take for granted (and thus no longer question). However, bear in mind that these textbooks are written by authors who are not necessarily self-reflective about the fundamental assumptions of their field (W.H. Newell, pers. comm., 3 December 2013). As a result, you may need at a certain point to articulate those assumptions and articulate other specific elements of a discipline in order to integrate its insights with those from other disciplines.

Other particularly helpful sources of information at the start of your literature research are review articles. In a review article, a researcher (or group of researchers) answers a research question or maps the state-of-the-art knowledge regarding a theme or a problem by analyzing and integrating the results of tens or sometimes even hundreds of relevant research articles. These review articles are a good source for getting an up-to-date overview of the perspectives within a field on a subject or problem.

With the knowledge you have now gained, you can refine your concept map into a more theoretically informed concept map. For example, take a look at figure 15, which presents a concept map concerning the subject of major depressive disorder.

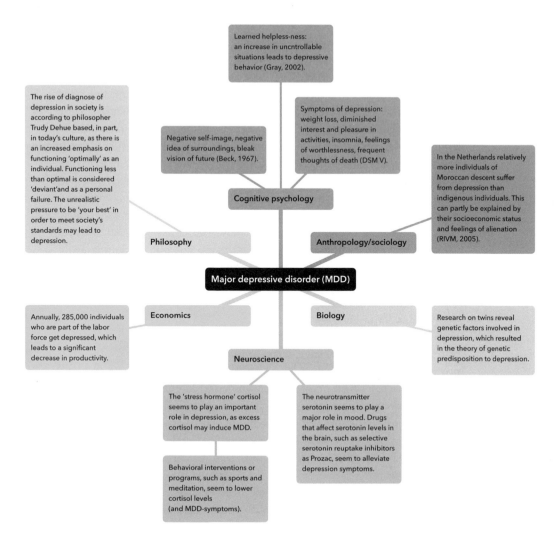

Figure 15   Concept map on Major Depressive Disorder (MDD)

Step 2   Formulate preliminary research question

At this point, you have decided on a topic, identified disciplines relevant to that topic, and created a concept map in which the main disciplinary theoretical perspectives are presented. This concept map will help you to formulate a preliminary research question. It is a preliminary research question because you will refine and adjust it according to the theoretical and methodological insights that you will gather when developing a theoretical framework (the next step in the research process; see figure 9). However, you do need a preliminary research question, as this will guide you to finding relevant theories and research in your fields of interest. Without a clear focus – a specific research question, in this case - on what you want to research within your topic of choice, it is easy to get lost in the vast amount of academic literature.

When setting up a preliminary research question, try to avoid specific disciplinary biases as they may complicate interdisciplinary collaboration and integration further down the road. If possible, at this early stage, avoid unnecessary jargon, technical terms, or even non-technical terms that are characteristically used by academics from one discipline. One way to avoid these disciplinary terms is to try to formulate the problem in everyday language. Do not get discouraged when the terms are vague or imprecise, because this may be an advantage, insofar as it admits multiple interpretations that may offer as many clues to different disciplines. Some researchers find it troublesome, for example, that there are many different definitions of consciousness, whereas others contend that, as a result, many different research approaches to consciousness are invited, which eventually might come together in a more complete explanation of this complex phenomenon. In other words, during subsequent steps of the interdisciplinary process, you will probably re-examine the definition of the problem, and develop more precise wording that is responsive to all the relevant perspectives (Newell, 2007).

Examples of research questions that are not reasonably narrowed down:

- How can we improve sustainable agriculture?
- Is the judiciary affected by criticism?
- What is the best cure for depression?

Problems with the previous research questions are, amongst others, that results from previous research, which are usually much more specific, have not been incorporated in the question (i.e. 'How can we improve sustainable agriculture?'), contain concepts that lack specificity (i.e. 'judiciary' and 'criticism') or ask for too many possible conditions to investigate (i.e. 'What is the best cure for depression?').

Examples of research questions that are reasonably narrowed down:

- To what extent can fogponics contribute to sustainable agriculture?
- What are the effects of societal and political criticism on the judiciary in the Netherlands?
- To what extent can the medication selective serotonine reuptake inhibitors (SSRIs) increase the effectiveness of cognitive behavioral therapy in patients diagnosed with depression?

Your ultimate research question has to meet more criteria. Although you will check later on, when you finalize your research question, whether your research question is relevant, anchored, researchable, and precise, it can help to have these criteria in the forefront of your mind when you work on your preliminary research question (see also figure 16). The goal is a finalized research question that is:

| **Relevant:** | It should be related to the broader problem you wish to address, reflect the reason for your research project, and be the driver for interdisciplinary research. In short, it should be clear why it is worthwhile to seek an answer to the question. |
| **Anchored:** | It should be the logical outcome of your literature review, expert interviews, and theoretical framework. Your research question has to be embedded in the fields of knowledge of your research topic, and the result should be of added value to the fields involved. |

| **Researchable:** | It should be possible to conceive research methods that can address the question in the amount of time and with the means available. |
| **Precise:** | It should be straightforward and specific. It should be clear what the research focus is. |

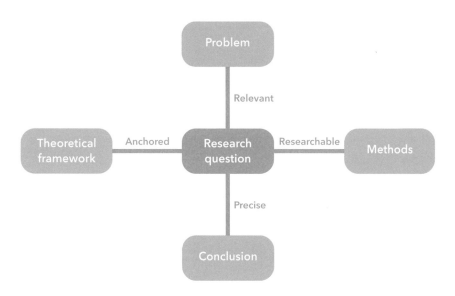

Figure 16   Defining characteristics of the research question: Relevant to the broader problem that is to be addressed, anchored in the theoretical framework, researchable with the methods at hand, and leading to a precise and straightforward conclusion

One more thing to keep in mind when developing a research question is that your finalized research question should incorporate all relevant perspectives. Try to avoid a one-sided question, for example by leaning too much to one discipline's theory. At the same time, you have to make sure that the question is not too general in nature and relates to a specific element of the topic.

9 Theoretical framework and research question[1]

It is now time to turn the preliminary research question into a researchable research question. By developing a theoretical framework that addresses your preliminary research question, you will be able to describe the 'state of the art' in your field of interest, sharpen your ideas, and then formulate a better, more specified research question. This part of the research process is described in this paragraph (and displayed in figure 17).

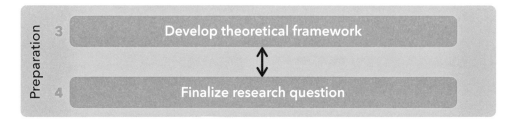

Figure 17   Steps 3 and 4 of the IIS Model for interdisciplinary research

Considerations:
- Consider all relevant theories, concepts, and assumptions that each discipline can contribute.
- Where do disciplinary theories overlap? Where can you find or create common ground?
- Is it possible to integrate the theoretical frameworks of the relevant disciplines?

As discussed in chapter 6, communication between (disciplinary) perspectives is a first important step towards integrating these perspectives. So an important question is how to enhance communication within your interdisciplinary research group? First and foremost, an understanding of one's own discipline is needed if a useful conversation between academics from different disciplines is to occur. In other words, one should be familiar with the theories, concepts, and methodologies that are central to one's discipline and realize how these and other ingredients make up

---

1   The authors thank Coyan Tromp for allowing them to make use of her work on data management tables in this chapter.

the Science Cycle according to which scientific research of your topic is conducted (see chapter 2 on what science is). One could also answer the following questions as a way of bringing the disciplinary perspective to the forefront (partly after Paul & Elder, 2014):

- What is your disciplinary perspective on the problem?
- Which insights is this perspective based on?
- What are the strengths and weaknesses of this perspective?
- What are the borders of your disciplinary perspective in researching the problem? That is to say: where do you see opportunities to collaborate with other disciplines?

The second and arguably the most important skill to enhance communication (and thus integration) across disciplines is critical self-reflection. Different methodologies to enhance conversation between academics of different disciplines have emerged, and they all stress the importance of academics' self-reflection on their (disciplinary) assumptions, mindset, and background. Lélé and Norgaard (2005), for example, emphasize that all researchers operate with implicit assumptions that are based on personal values and are guided by their discipline, to the exclusion of others. Reflecting on your personal values and assumptions can be a daunting task: how can you reflect on ideas you may not hold on a conscious level? You could think of the following types of questions to uncover your own or your colleagues' personal and disciplinary assumptions (based on the Socratic method):

- Questions aimed at clarification ('Can you explain...?')
- Questions to test assumptions ('How can you verify or falsify that assumption?')
- Questions that determine the argumentation ('Can there be a reason to question this evidence?')
- Questions to explore alternative perspectives ('Can someone else have a different perspective on this?')
- Questions that determine implications and consequences ('What would happen if...?')
- Questions that question the question ('What is the goal of this question?')

Thirdly, as explained in chapter 6, a main precondition for interdisciplinary integration is the ability of researchers to explain their different backgrounds, perspectives, and insights into the research problem. Practically, this means one has to be able to articulate and communicate one's perspective in a way that someone who does not share this specific disciplinary background can comprehend. For example, when explaining one's perspective, avoid using jargon or technical terms. It also means, when a colleague from another discipline is explaining her perspective, one has to dare to ask (critical) questions. Critical, open, and respectful communication with academics from other disciplines is one way to discover the assumptions underlying a discipline. This may be harder for solo interdisciplinarians, who may uncover disciplinary assumptions by observing cognitive dissonance, parsing a problem into components, critical thinking, and other modes of intellectual problem solving (W.H. Newell, pers. comm., 3 December 2013).

When engaging in communication with someone from another field, it can be useful to consider the following questions regarding the way someone else is communicating her perspective (after Paul & Elder, 2014):

■ Does the researcher clarify key concepts when necessary? Are the concepts used justifiably?
■ Does the researcher show sensitivity to what she is taking for granted or assuming?
■ Does the researcher use questionable assumptions without addressing problems which might be inherent in those assumptions?
■ Does the researcher show sensitivity to alternative relevant points of view or lines of reasoning? Does she consider and respond to objections framed from other relevant points of view?

Step 3   Develop theoretical framework

With the preliminary research question in mind, you have to do literature research in order to develop a theoretical framework. Such a framework can be defined as a comprehensive explanation of some aspect of the natural or social world that is supported by a vast body of evidence, generating testable and falsifiable predictions. This theoretical framework can serve as the 'backbone' of your research question and will help you to select the information or knowledge that is most relevant for your research. In addition, it can help you identify the most useful methods for studying this topic.

Note that the development of a theoretical framework is an ongoing process: you will be working on the framework throughout (the first half of) your research project. As your research progresses and you learn more about the research topic, you will also need to update your theoretical framework. This means that you have to constantly switch (or iterate) between your research question (and sub-questions), your theoretical framework, and your methods. Your integrated theoretical framework will ultimately be a substantial part of your research proposal and final report. In addition, by constructing it early in the research process, it can also serve as a tool for developing a relevant and firmly anchored research question. The following tasks are important in creating a theoretical framework:

■ Collecting disciplinary insights into the problem.
■ Analyzing the nature of differences between these insights.
■ Finding or creating common ground through the use of different integration techniques.

Below we explain in more detail what these tasks entail.

It is important to have an overview of the research in your field of interest. To gain insight into the 'state of the art' of the relevant disciplines, you will need to find out which ideas and theories have already been developed through research within these different disciplines. Academic disciplines organize and store their knowledge by means of specific journals and databases. So make sure you list the major journals and publications within the fields that are relevant to your research project. Another good starting point is an interview with an expert on the topic. An expert can help you to refine your literature search and choose the most relevant perspectives to research a topic.

In order to begin constructing an integrated theoretical framework, you may need to create several more specific theoretical frameworks from different disciplines before you are able to decide on how to integrate their most relevant parts. The integrated theoretical framework should:

- offer a critical overview of relevant academic literature on your research topic and question;
- be based on perspectives and theories from each of the selected disciplines, preferably from more than one field (or sub-discipline) within each discipline;
- be a coherent story, as opposed to just a collection of concepts or theories, and show the reasoning behind the integrated perspectives that led to your research question.

For example, in the research project on fogponics (chapter 12) several theoretical frameworks pertaining to different disciplines had to be integrated in order to be able to address the research question: To what extent can fogponics contribute to sustainable agriculture? First, the students defined sustainable development as encompassing both environmental and economic stakes or needs, and they chose to focus on tomato plants and their nutrient and water use (based on insights from economics that tomatoes are an important export product for the Netherlands). Biologists had developed fogponics systems (where 'hanging' roots are provided with water in the form of fog), whereas chemists had developed a system that could help by measuring the use of nutrients (the so-called HPLC technique). Using additional theoretical frameworks from mathematics and artificial intelligence, the students could respectively simulate plant growth (to make comparisons to current greenhouse culture) and make the fogponics system as efficient as possible.

A useful tool for comparing disciplinary insights and understanding their basis is a data management table (after Repko, 2008; see figure 18), which lists the assumptions, theories, and methods of research from the relevant disciplinary literature on the subject. A data management table not only provides an overview of the relevant disciplinary insights into the research problem, later on in the research project it can also provide a basis for interdisciplinary integration at both the theoretical and the methodological level. Moreover, it provides an extremely useful tool for a team of researchers to assemble the ingredients that individual team members will be collecting.

Full reference to the book or article				
Discipline / sub-discipline	Theory / hypothesis	Concept(s)	Assumptions / methodology	Insight into problem
Name the specific research field and specialization.	Explain what it entails; describe the relation between the (f) actors that are considered or conjectured to be relevant (e.g. cause X and effects Y + Z, or the correlation between different (f)actors; or why a certain intervention is thought to be useful in helping to overcome the problem).	Analyze the key building blocks of the explanation or conceptualization captured in the theoretical framework. Give clear definitions of them. Explain which of the (potentially plural) definitions you will take as a point of departure in your research project.	Analyze the basic assumptions underlying your theoretical framework. Those assumptions can have an ontological, epistemological, methodological, or cultural philosophical nature, i.e. they can be related to our views on reality, and to our views on how we can gain knowledge about that reality, how we can best study that reality, and about how science can contribute to society. Explain which assumptions you will incorporate, or which you reject.	Explain how the theory and the key concepts it entails help to provide more insight in or a possible solution to the problem you are addressing. Take also into consideration possible limitations.

Figure 18   Data management table

How can you find the relevant research fields, theories, concepts, and assumptions for your interdisciplinary research? Below we provide a list indicating where you may find the various elements of the data management table.

Discipline / sub-discipline

To find out which discipline the insights you find useful for your research are coming from, the following questions may help:

- Check the title of the journal; what kind of research field is represented in the title?
- Check the affiliation of author(s). What kind of institution(s) or organization(s) are they working for? If you are not sure, look further on the internet to find more information about the author(s).
- Similarly, check the reference list attached to the article for prominent journal and book titles and other indications of their disciplinary backgrounds.
- Check the mind map you made when working on your preliminary research question. What research fields are linked to your problem?

Theory

Finding out which theory lies at the basis of the insights you find useful can be hard. Here, we provide some advice on how to uncover it:

- Sometimes a prominent theory or hypothesis is explicitly named in an article, like the theory of evolution, the Marxist theory, or the Goldbach conjecture. It might even be taken up in the abstract. Then, it is only a matter of looking for a good description of what the theory states or, if you cannot find one in the article or book, to try and formulate it yourself.
  (Note: theories can be closely related to concepts. For tips on how to identify key concepts, see below.)

- When the theory is not explicitly stated in the article, it can usually be found in review articles. These types of articles not only provide the state-of-the-art theories in the research field, they often present and compare a variety of possible explanations. These alternative explanations may be similar, analogous explanations, but they may also be completely different and thus form a competitor for the theory favored by the particular research group whose article or book you are reading.

- Another strategy for finding out about what theory the author(s) adhere to is to try and find online information about the author(s) (see the suggestion above under 'discipline-sub-discipline').

- It may be helpful to make a theory map in which you summarize all the answers you have found about what exactly the theory entails, how it came into being, who coined the name, what contribution the theory can make to the field under study and, specifically, to your research topic, whether any data were found to support the theory, and what alternative and competitive interpretations exist.

Concepts

To identify the concepts that are relevant to your research project, the following guidelines are useful:

- Concepts answer the 'what' question: what is the research project about, i.e. what are the phenomena under investigation? To find the concepts, think of keywords that are also often listed on the first page of journal articles.

- Concepts often contain special, unusual terms and jargon. This is not always the case though; sometimes a common word is used in a particular way. That is why giving a clear definition of a concept is very important.

- The 'same' concept can often be found in different theories and different researchers might use them in the context of different theoretical frameworks, and may thus give different interpretations of such a concept. This holds for rationality, chaos and equilibrium, for example.

- Concepts can sometimes be difficult to distinguish from theories, principles, causal links, phenomena, or methods. It might help you to realize that a theory is an overarching framework and a concept is one of the defining key elements within that theory. But when the concept of, for instance, resilience is considered to be such a key driver that researchers start talking about resilience theory, the distinction obviously becomes a bit blurred.

- 'Concept' is sometimes even used in a still broader sense, in the sense of approach or discourse.
- Just as with theories, it can be helpful to create a concept map in which you summarize all the answers you have found about what the concept exactly is, how it came into being, who coined the name, what contribution the concept can make to the theories in the field and, specifically, with regard to your research topic, whether any data were found to support the meaning and role of the concept, and what alternative and competitive interpretations exist of one and the 'same' concept.

Assumptions

The assumptions underlying a discipline are often implicit as scientists within a field share them without questioning these assumptions. Making these assumptions explicit can help to articulate differences or conflicts between disciplines – and scientists – and sometimes even to remove them. There are various kinds of assumptions:

- Ontological assumptions, concerning what is considered real and what not. Disciplines differ with respect to what they consider the building blocks (constituents) or reality and what they consider to be mere appearances. The ontological status of mathematical objects can be disputed, or of survival value, or of antimatter, or of consciousness, to give a few examples.
- Epistemological assumptions concern the question what can be known, and what not. Knowledge can be considered a valid 'mirror of reality', whereas others might think of knowledge as a mere instrument that works, or not, with yet others remaining quite skeptical about the nature and value of knowledge in general.
- Anthropological assumptions pertain to what it is to be human and about human needs, fears, values and the like. Such assumptions might be relevant for how scientists think about humans as their object of knowledge but also about their own position as scientists.
- Cultural and social assumptions often matter as well, as science is both a product of culture and society and produces results with an impact on these. Depending on how disciplines or scientists conceive of culture and society, they may reflect differently upon what science is and how it should function. The concept of the 'knowledge society' is based upon the assumption that knowledge and knowledge production is fundamental to our current society – which can be debated.
- Ethical assumptions are relevant when it comes to deciding about what scientific questions merits attention and money, choosing how to conduct a research project and especially about the implementation of scientific results. The use of science and scientific results by the military and in irresponsible environmental and social projects has led to questions about 'dual use' of these results and about the ethical neutrality of science and scientists.
- Methodological assumptions refer to implicit ideas about research strategies, methods for experimentation and analysis, and the like. Scientists can silently assume that their colleagues share their ideas about valid and objective methods,

even though all scientific methods have their limitations in terms of validity, objectivity, feasibility, and so on. Inter- and transdisciplinary research almost always uses a methodological pluralism, which requires scientists to articulate and reconsider these assumptions.

These kinds of assumptions are among the most relevant in the context of science. Note that we do not argue against having such assumptions: It is not wrong to implicitly assume that nature's laws will be the same tomorrow as they are today, for example, as it would be useless to do research if a scientist thought otherwise. Articulating and doubting this assumption about the behavior of the laws of nature is usually unnecessary. However, as Einstein's critique of Newton's law of gravity has shown, even a natural law might turn out to be conditional in ways that were previously unthinkable. In other words, the ontological assumption about material reality being unconditionally determined by a particular law-like relation turned out to be in need of revision. Similarly, the physicists assuming that the knowledge concerning this law was complete had to recognize the incorrectness of their assumption. Given its central role in Newtonian physics, the reconsideration and partial rejection of this assumption was a difficult process. Similar processes have taken place in other disciplines as well. Other examples are Darwin's rejection of the assumed purposeful nature of the evolution of natural kinds, or the rejection by behavioral economists of the assumption that economic decisions are always rational and not influenced by emotions.

It is good to realize that the critique of 'normal science' – in Kuhn's terms (see chapter 3) – often targets such assumptions and that scientific breakthroughs often consist of the rejection of an assumption that is implicitly accepted by a scientific community. Not all interdisciplinary or transdisciplinary research projects are revolutionary in this sense, obviously, yet they still require the articulation, discussion, and reconsideration of relevant assumptions by the team members. It is very helpful to use a data management table when doing so as you are required to articulate such assumptions that implicitly structure the disciplinary research being integrated in the project.

Below is an example of a data management table filled in with information on disciplinary research on the link between alcohol consumption and aggressive behavior.

Caetano, R., Schafer, J. & Cunradi, C.B. (2001). Alcohol-related intimate partner violence among White, Black, and Hispanic couples in the United States. Alcohol Research and Health, 25, 58-65

Discipline / sub-discipline	Theory / hypothesis	Concept(s)	Assumptions / methodology	Insight into problem
Psychology: Understanding behavior and mental processes of individuals by researching both groups of people and specific cases	**Subculture of violence theory:** Certain groups in society accept violence as a means of conflict resolution more than other groups **Social structure theory:** Socioeconomic factors that characterize the lives of specific groups	**Intimate Partner Violence (IPV):** Male-to-female/ female-to-male intimate partner violence **Violence:** 11 (physical) violence items from the Conflict Tactics Scale: throwing, pushing, grabbing, shoving, slapping, kicking, biting, hitting, beating-up, choking, burning, forcing sex, threatening with knife or gun, stabbing, and/or shooting	**Higher rate found among female-to-male IPV:** May be due to underreporting of violence data across gender or because in clinical samples men are more violent **Coding alcohol consumption:** More than three drinks a day considered heavy drinking	**Support for the subculture of violence theory:** Black subjects reported significantly higher female-to-male IPV (not male-to female IPV) than White subjects when controlled for factors such as socioeconomic background, drinking, and history of victimization The presence of drinking in an IPV incident does not mean that alcohol is the cause of the violence; it may also be explained by the **expectation that alcohol will disinhibit,** or that some people use **alcohol as an excuse**
Epidemiology: The study of patterns of health and illness and associated factors at the population level, identifying risk factors (for disease) and determining optimal treatment approaches to clinical practice and for preventive measures	**Acute effects hypothesis:** Alcohol disinhibits aggressive behavior **Alcohol as excuse hypothesis** Alcohol is a convenient factor to excuse behavior that would otherwise be unacceptable **Chronic effects hypothesis:** People with a history of heavy drinking are predisposed to violence or drinking heavily (which leads to violence) due to other factors or have alcohol-exacerbated brain damage associated with violent outbursts	**Alcohol problem measures:** Survey with 29 alcohol-related problems from 14 specific problem areas **Problem syndrome:** Clustering of problems in one area (e.g., alcohol dependence) with other factors (e.g., IPV); socio-demographic factors and psychosocial variables	**Sample is representative** and can be applied to all couples in US but not to couples with alcohol-related problems that are uncommon **The sample is limited:** Mostly 'moderate' violence in household sample, and showing only associations, not causations **Coding ethnicity:** Black Hispanic, White Hispanic, Black not Hispanic, White not Hispanic (no mixed category) **Violence:** Unreported violence does not count. Only reported physical violence not emotional abuse	Individual level factors, characteristics of the relationship, and characteristics of the environment (social structure) form a constellation of factors resulting in IPV Alcohol problems not always cause of IPV, but can be used as **marker for identifying population at (more) risk of IPV**

Figure 19   Example of a data management table

Fish, E.W, Faccidomo, S. & Miczek, K.A. (1999). Aggression heightened by alcohol or social instigation in mice: Reduction by the 5-HT B receptor agonist CP-94,253. *Psychopharmacology*, 146, 391-399

Discipline / sub-discipline	Theory / hypothesis	Concept(s)	Assumptions / methodology	Insight into problem
Behavioural neuroscience: The study of physiological and developmental mechanisms of behavior in humans and animals **Neurochemistry:** The study of neurochemicals (molecules such as neurotransmitters) that influence networks of neural operation **Genetics:** The study of genetic variation, specific genes and heredity in organisms	**Individual differences in brain chemistry can predict behavior:** Psychopathological behavior can be treated clinically with medicine (agonists that mimic naturally occurring substances) based on knowledge of the brain's molecular receptors **Genes affect behavior:** It has been found that individuals with a genetic predisposition to drink alcohol exhibit tendencies towards impulsive violent behavior	**Receptor and agonist:** An agonist is a chemical that binds to a receptor of a cell and triggers a response by the cell. An agonist often mimics the action of a naturally occurring substance	**The treatment works on curtailing this behaviour** Pharmacological agents toward this serotonin-receptor subtype may have more behaviourally specific anti-aggressive effects than those of other current treatments **Animal models do not transfer to human trials completely** The 5-HT1B receptors are not identical in rodents and humans, but functionally homologous **Genetic modification affects behavior via neurochemicals** Mice, in which the gene that codes for 5-HT1B receptors has been 'knocked out', show aggressive behavior	**Social context also impacts behavior** • The activation of the 5-HT1B serotonin receptor subtype preferentially attenuates heightened aggression due to social instigation or alcohol treatment (in mice) • The social stimuli that precede and occur during an aggressive encounter potently modulate aggressive arousal **Biological correlates of behavior might explain some differences in aggression between individuals** Neurochemically, aggressive arousal seems to be particularly related to the inhibition of serotonin. Knock-out mice lacking the gene for the 5-HT1B receptor attack faster and have higher frequencies of attack bites **The same amount of alcohol affects different people differently** In mice, only a subgroup (20%) show robust and reliable enhancement of aggressive behaviors at 1.0 g/kg dose of alcohol **Conclusion (insights from mice into the human experience):** There may be a genetic component for aggressive behavior that is elevated by alcohol, and both aggressive behavior and alcohol intake may be influenced by serotonin. Also, linkage has been found between antisocial alcoholics and polymorphisms at the 5-HT 1B gene

Figure 20   Example of a data management table

As you explore the literature, make sure to update your data management table repeatedly throughout the process and to always share it as a team with each other. This not only means that you should keep adding information and insights to your table, but you should also remove irrelevant insights from earlier research phases and keep these in a separate table. Ultimately, your combined data management table will consist of a good coverage of the research topic, including each relevant disciplinary perspective. The items in the table should also make visible to you those places where disciplinary insights are lacking or unclear. It is at this point that students often find a fruitful, focused question for their research to address.

2   Analysis of differences and conflicts

Using a data management table will not only enable you to detect harmonious insights from different disciplines in the literature. Perhaps more importantly, it will help to discover insights that conflict with each other. These conflicting insights can offer you an opportunity for interdisciplinary integration, as you will see below. The following questions can help in finding conflicting and supporting insights:

- Do the insights of different disciplines center around the same topic about which they reveal different aspects?
- Do some of these insights support each other?
- Preferably, insights that support each other should stem from different lines of research and thus rely upon methodological pluralism. For example, children with ADHD have academic difficulties as they have lower average school marks and score lower on attention span tasks.
- In what specific ways do the disciplinary insights contradict or differ from each other?

For example, are the apparent contradictions between results perhaps due to the fact that the insights are derived from studies with different age groups or in different countries? That might point to a developmental influence or a cultural or social one, which might facilitate your more comprehensive interdisciplinary understanding.

Once you have established if there are differences between disciplinary insights, the challenge is to investigate the nature of the differences (after Repko, 2008). One can ask the following questions to discover this:

- Do the disciplinary perspectives use the same concept yet mean something different?
- How are concepts defined and measured?
- Do the different disciplinary theories rest on different assumptions?
- Do these assumptions conflict with each other or can they be seen as complementary?
- Can the conflict between insights be attributed to the different conditions of the research?

In the example of the theoretical analysis of the two articles in the data management table (see box 6), there are tensions between two approaches that rather focus on 'nurture' (social/epidemiological) or on 'nature' (biological/neurological). Questions arise about the extent to which the findings in animal research can be translated to humans (to what extent are the effects of alcohol in the brain of a rat comparable to the effects in a human brain?). Other differences can be found in how aggression is defined and in what amount of alcohol intake is considered problematic. Mind you, this is only a selection of issues that make the insights from the different perspectives at first sight 'incommensurable'. If you were to start scrutinizing the methods (see the chapter on methods), you would find more conflicting operationalizations of concepts and methodological assumptions.

> **Box 6**
>
> ## Alcohol consumption and aggressive behavior – analysis of the data management table
>
> Suppose that your topic of interest is why alcoholics are often more abusive toward their family members than toward others.
>
> The first article reviews several theories on alcohol-related intimate partner violence among White, Black, and Hispanic partners. Apparently, alcohol consumption goes hand in hand with increases in aggressive behaviour toward partners. It is unclear, however, whether alcohol should be considered the cause of aggression. Certain expectations, individual and relationship history, and environmental factors also seem to play a role when violence occurs.
>
> The authors of the second article discuss social instigation or social stimuli that precede the violence, and they address variants in brain receptors that somehow modulate the level of aggressiveness.
>
> At first glance, the different insights all seem to provide a piece of the puzzle that you are trying to solve. But problems could lurk below the surface, such as:
>
> 1 Do both articles adhere to the same concept of violence?
>   • Does this match your preconceived definition of violence?
> 2 What level of alcohol consumption are both articles talking about?
>   • How does that compare to the 'alcoholics' you want to study?
> 3 Do the articles favor the social correlates of violence over the neural correlates, or is it the other way around?
>   • In the first article, the level of analysis of brain biochemistry is not considered to be relevant to the behaviour under study. In the second article, however, the social circumstances modulate aggressive arousal in the brain; this modulation is described in biochemical terms, without a mention of individual or social history.
> 4 Animal studies vs. studies with humans.
>   • The second article does experiments with mice, whereas the first deals with human subjects. Are the 'mouse insights' relevant to understanding the human condition?

Once you have gathered insights into the topic you are researching from all relevant disciplines, it is time to take the first steps toward an interdisciplinary understanding of this topic: what is the common ground between various insights from diverse disciplines? This will form the basis for interdisciplinary integration and also allows you to redefine your main research question in an interdisciplinary way. Remember that such interdisciplinary integration not only involves pertinent techniques but can also require creative imagination for the development of a novel explanatory mechanism, a novel intervention, a novel technology, and so on. We do not have the space here to deal exhaustively with all possible kinds of common ground or all integration techniques that might be used, but hope that our treatment is sufficient to be both helpful and perhaps inspiring for the creative imagination you need as a scientist.

As much as you need to discover an overlap in interests when developing a topic for your interdisciplinary research, you should also try to find common ground when developing an interdisciplinary insight into it. Finding common ground can occur along different lines but often involves: (i) pinpointing a key theory or insight that is somehow shared between disciplines but may be defined and operationalized in different ways; and/or (ii) elaborating an explanatory mechanism by integrating additional insights into it; and/or (iii) making assumptions explicit that might need to be reconsidered by one or more disciplines; and/or (iv) realizing that an existing methodology can perhaps be improved using insights from other disciplines; and/or (v) realizing that the apparently contrasting results from different studies can be reinterpreted in such a way that they are consistent with each other. In some cases, (vi) common ground is created by an existing intervention that must be made more robust by adjusting it in response to a newly uncovered additional factor.

Here are some examples of finding common ground. Some sciences share a common ground right from the beginning in the form of a comprehensive theory, which might need further elaboration in order to explain a particular phenomenon. For example, the theory of quantum mechanics is shared between fields as diverse as astronomy, physics and biology, facilitating to some extent their collaboration. We already discussed how a complex mechanistic explanation allows integration of varied types of explanation. Earlier we also mentioned how economists and sociologists found common ground when they reconsidered the assumption that individuals always maximize their economic self-interest, which made it difficult to explain certain forms of sacrifice or altruism. Contrasting results can sometimes be made consistent with each other once researchers realize that their focus was actually on different developmental stages of a phenomenon or that a particular difference between the study populations was in fact influencing the outcomes in an unexpected manner. Finally, methodologies are often developed within a certain field but turn out to be valuable in others, as when remote sensing has yielded many benefits outside geography in fields like archaeology, astronomy, and sociology.

Although you might have found common ground between disciplines, you should not expect that the tensions between elements of the different disciplines are now completely solved. Instead, it may be useful to focus on these remaining interdisciplinary tensions, as this can lead you to formulate a new question and gain a novel, more comprehensive insight (see box 7). The example on alcohol consumption and aggression presented earlier implies that simply taking the disciplinary insights at face value and building your theoretical framework purely on that basis would lead to a multidisciplinary collage but not to new, integrated interdisciplinary insights. So, although dissecting the nature of differences may feel like a counterintuitive and even counterproductive approach (why would you not focus on where insights overlap or support each other?), focusing on the tensions between research results can provide valuable insights into where common ground can be created.

Especially among the humanities and the social sciences it is more likely that you have to create common ground. This has to do with the theoretical and methodological pluralism that reign in their domains more than in other domains, as mentioned earlier. Harmonious insights are few and differing, whereas conflicting (even diametrically opposed) and incommensurate (when the humanities are added) insights are common. Moreover, in addition to their dependence upon different epistemological assumptions (i.e. if something exists, how can you know that?), these non-harmonious insights usually also stem from different ontological assumptions (what can be said to really exist?) (W.H. Newell, pers. comm., 3 December 2013). Again, such differences between disciplines or specific theories within a discipline regarding their assumptions can offer as many ways to find common ground between them.

Within sociology, for example, authors like Herbert Marcus and Erich Fromm have developed accounts of human society and psychology in which both competing Marxist and psychoanalytical theories were incorporated. The authors dismantled the theories from their exclusivist claims before they could integrate them into accounts of human society and psychology. They argued that a capitalist society with a strong emphasis on consumerism has an impact on the development of certain psychological attitudes in individuals.

Obviously, if one is creating common ground by adjusting the assumptions that underlie certain theories or methods, it is often necessary to reconsider other elements as well. This is due to the fact that many of the ingredients of a science depend upon each other – which is captured by the term 'paradigm' as we have seen above. The challenge is therefore to modify concepts or assumptions as little as possible when bringing out latent commonalities (Newell, 2007).

In this chapter, we have referred to different ways of finding and creating common ground. It is important to realize that, in most cases, we are in fact discussing the different integration techniques that were presented in chapter 6. Remember that these techniques implied that one could use the different techniques of adding, adjusting, or connecting by applying them to scientific theories, methods, or results. We will close this chapter by listing some questions that might help you and your team to embark on this important yet difficult process of finding and creating common ground. You might start to answer these – and more – questions individually and then discuss your answers together, looking for potential connections and overlaps between them.

- Which theories and elements of those theories do you think are most relevant to look into for your research topic?
- Can you discover connections and overlaps of those theories and their elements with those of other disciplines?
- How would you operationalize research into the relevant component(s) or process(es)? How would you study them? What methods, subjects, instruments etc. would you use? Give multiple options if possible.
- Could you articulate the implicit assumptions that are made in your discipline regarding theoretical or methodological elements? Could you imagine different definitions of central concepts, for example? Or would an unusual method of research be potentially interesting?
- What definitions of concepts and elements are central to your approach to the research topic? Do you think that another discipline shares these definitions or might have alternative definitions?
- How do the other disciplines investigate your research topic? Could their methods, subjects, instruments, etc. be added to those of your discipline or are they focusing on different components or processes?
- Do you think that certain components or processes form a coherent subcomponent or, instead, that a certain component should be separated into two or more independent components? Could this explain how the results of a particular study are related to those of a study in another discipline?
- Is there a developmental or historical episode that you think has been neglected while it is relevant for your research topic? Could adding a historical element to an explanatory theory solve this hiatus?
- Similarly, is there a contextual, external, or environmental factor that merits more study as it might have a decisive impact on your research topic?
- Is there a particular intervention that might affect your research topic in a decisive way and that deserves to be better understood?

After having thought about such questions individually and as a group, discuss in your group what you thought of and apply any necessary changes to the map.

Different disciplinary definitions: An example

Three students from the fields of biology, cognitive science, and artificial intelligence decided that they wanted to know whether a new monitoring device that could measure stress levels would also be effective in reducing an individual's stress level (Olthof, Bulters & Zwennes, 2011). After reading several articles, they noticed that the concept of 'stress' is defined differently from different disciplinary theoretical perspectives.

From the perspective of artificial intelligence, stress is defined as an objective, measurable factor. The sudden presence of sweat on the skin and an increased heart rate are seen as indicative of stress. Biologists define stress as an external trigger that causes changes in hormone levels and other complex processes that upset 'homeostasis', which are factors that are hard to measure directly. Cognitive science defines stress as a brain state that can occur below the level of conscious perception. Thus, brain states triggered by stressful events are also hard to measure.

From the definitions above, it is possible to see that although stress was a shared concept, it would only provide common ground if the tension between 'externally measurable stress' and 'internal non-measurable processes of stress responses and their interpretation' could be relieved. The research group thus decided that the user of the stress monitor would need to be able to communicate with the stress monitor, for example by temporarily changing settings in hot weather or when doing exercise. AI's assumption that external measurements of stress-related proxies would be objective had to be dropped. Simply monitoring would probably not be sufficient; to be of service in stress reduction both device and human subject are needed in the monitoring process.

In sum, insights derived from different disciplines often appear to be incommensurate, conflicting, or diametrically opposed. The foundation of interdisciplinary integration is the awareness that a discipline operates on specific assumptions, concepts, and theories, and that these differ from discipline to discipline. Through the willingness to embrace 'the new' and the identification of shared concerns, the challenge of interdisciplinary integration can be faced (see the example in box 8).

Box 8

Interdisciplinary integration in practice: How to speak 'economish'

When Eldar Shafir (Princeton) and Sendhil Mullainathan (Harvard), researchers in psychology and economics, respectively, started to work on a theory of poverty, they spent a lot of time creating a common language. Shafir: "Tolerance, openness, and non-defensiveness of your field are crucial. The goal is to speak the same language, understand each other's issues and perspective. Take Jerry Fodor and Noam Chomsky. They've been talking to each other for so many years that it's hard to say who's the linguist and who's the philosopher" (E. Shafir, pers. comm., 12 December 2013).

As a psychologist, Shafir has invested a lot of time in understanding the economist's perspective. "I wasn't so much interested in the equations; I was trying to figure out what assumptions they had about people. What is the human agent in the eye of the economist? You have to appreciate the other's perspective in order to succeed in interdisciplinary work."

A well-justified transfer of ideas from one discipline to another may also enhance the insights from the disciplines. More practical techniques of integration are also possible; these are discussed later on when we elaborate upon the methodological challenges of conducting interdisciplinary research. Below, in box 9, you will find examples of integration in students' research projects through connecting theories, concepts, and assumptions.

Box 9
Examples of integration in students' research projects

Connecting theories and concepts
Power and dependency
In the field of development studies, power relations and dependencies are often analyzed in an international context, for example through use of dependency theory: A core of wealthy states benefits from resources flowing from peripheral countries, creating an interconnected world system.
In a research project about development and power relations, a student educated in interdisciplinary social sciences connected dependency theory to theories on power from other disciplines. He discovered that power could be analyzed at a global, international level, at an interpersonal level, and at a personal level. These levels are interdependent, meaning the actual effects of power relations at the global level influence the power relations at the interpersonal level, and vice versa. He therefore decided to develop a methodology that would enable him to take these interdependencies into account (Schram, 2012).

Connecting concepts and assumptions
Development and implementation of smart grids
When students were conducting a study into the use of sustainable and efficient electricity networks called smart grids, they realized that the experts in charge of developing and implementing a smart grid system on a student campus were from different disciplines. The economists wanted a solution based on the free market system, the physicists wanted to improve the state of the technology, and the psychologists wanted a solution that promoted human responsibility (Beukenhorst, Huygen & Van Leeuwen, 2012). By placing these assumptions as positions on a scale of possibilities, a spectrum appears: at one end, the state of the art of the technological system dictates the solution, and humans and the market follow; at the other end, the market selects, and humans and technology follow. In the middle, human parties can take responsibility for the development of the technological system and the way selection takes place in the market. So, the place where most of the expertise lies in the provision of the solution depends on the phase of product development and selection.

▼

In response to the incongruences of the solutions posed, the students changed their research question. They now asked what the demands of students (as compared to non-students) are with regard to their use of electricity, and whether they are more motivated by having the latest in technology, by financial stimuli, or by personal values, and what the outcome would mean to the development and implementation of smart grids on campuses. This new approach found common ground in a seemingly divergent problem and provided information that all three groups of experts could use to guide their decision making.

Connecting insights through a mechanistic model
Pelsser's food and behavior diet and ADHD

In order to investigate whether Pelsser's food and behavior diet is more effective than common treatments for ADHD, such as medication and parental training (or a combination of such treatments), three students in psychobiology, politicology, and pedagogy used an existing model from a handbook for the diagnosis and treatment of ADHD (Barkley, 2006) as common ground (Cederhout, Dodu & Perrin, 2012).

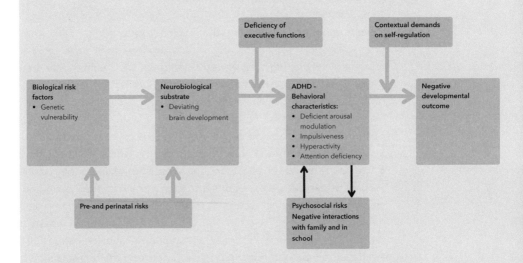

They expanded the model with theories on food-related ADHD and with insights into where in the model the different treatments could be expected to have an effect.

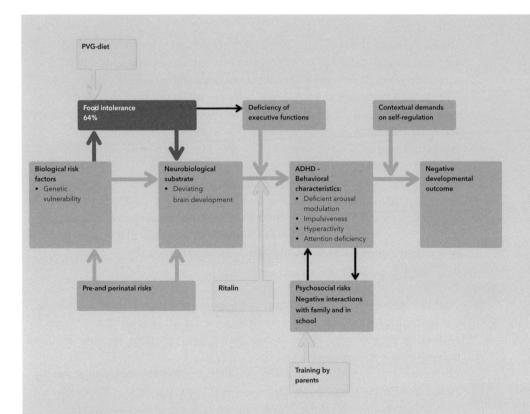

Through this integration, they could refocus their research question, and devise a method by which they reached the conclusion (i.e. new insight). They concluded that although the diet is effective when followed for about a year, and although it has no negative side-effects, only a limited group of children can really benefit from it; these are children in whom ADHD is indeed induced by food and whose parents are sufficiently motivated and disciplined to ensure that their children follow the diet.

Adding or 'borrowing' insights
Redlining and labor mobility

Redlining is a concept that refers to discriminating practices against people from a specific geographical area. An interdisciplinary social sciences student specialized in urban studies found that studies on redlining often try to find out whether it plays a role as a selection criterion in job interviews. She discovered that few studies focused on the perspective of individuals who are subjected to redlining. Combining insights (from human geography) into disadvantaged neighborhoods with theories (from social psychology) on stigmatization at a personal level, enabled her to generate insights into the consequences of redlining (Elands, 2011).

Step 4   Finalize research question

Through the use of one or more integration techniques, you were able to find common ground and develop an integrated theoretical framework. Based on these preliminary insights and the potential common ground between them, you can formulate an interdisciplinary research question, which will form the core of your research project. Make sure your research question is relevant, precise, researchable, and anchored (for more on these criteria, see chapter 9).

It is perhaps superfluous to note, but once your literature research becomes more focused and you have a workable research question, it is still advisable to keep updating your data management table. Along the way, you will find new valuable articles that help to specify and refine your data management table, and may be an incentive for a reformulation of your research question. As mentioned before, interdisciplinary research is an iterative process and it is likely that you will return to your research question and adjust it after every new step you take.

Step 5   Formulate sub-questions

Once you have finalized your research question, you will most likely have to divide this research question into sub-questions. For the sub-questions, the same criteria apply as for the research question (see chapter 9); however, there are some additional factors you have to consider.

There are two main factors you have to consider when developing sub-questions. First, it is important that the intended answers to the sub-questions together lead to an answer to the main research question. Perhaps you need to add another sub-question, if you have discovered that a previously undiscovered property or feature might have an impact upon the topic of your research. Adjust your sub-questions until they cover the finalized research question completely. Second, make sure that your sub-questions are logical steps that lead to your answer. Usually, you can answer one sub-question per paragraph.

For example, when dividing your research question into sub-questions, you can decide to divide a concept into terms that can be measured more easily. In the example on fogponics (chapter 13), the finalized research question 'To what extent can fogponics contribute to a more sustainable form of greenhouse cultivation?' is sub-divided into two questions:

- Is fogponics a better alternative in terms of efficient nutrient use when compared to conventional greenhouse agriculture?
- Is fogponics a better alternative in terms of efficient water use when compared to conventional greenhouse agriculture?

The sub-questions themselves can be divided into questions. In the example of fogponics one could research per nutrient whether fogponics or conventional greenhouse agriculture is a better alternative. However, be careful not to go overboard in sub-dividing your sub-questions, as this can lead to results that are redundant or too specific.

10 How to collect and analyze your data

After reviewing the relevant literature from the disciplines that were identified as being essential for addressing your initial research question, you have developed a theoretical framework that enabled you to refine the research question. Now, the question is, how are you going to answer this refined research question? It is time to develop a methodological framework for data collection and data analysis.

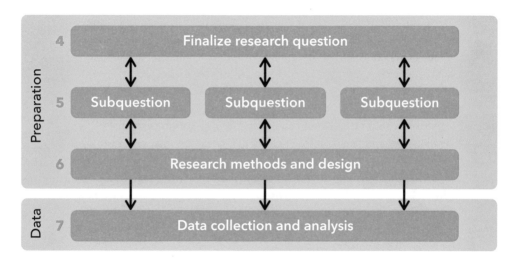

Figure 21   Steps 4, 5, 6 and 7 of the IIS model for interdisciplinary research

Considerations:
- What are the relevant methods each discipline has to offer? Is a combination of methods possible?
- How does the choice of methods influence the results?

Step 6   Develop research methods and design

The process of developing such a methodological framework to structure the practical matters of your research project is similar to the process you used to develop a theoretical framework to define the theoretical context and specify the focus of your research. This methodological framework is what we call 'the design' of your research. The process of translating your research questions into practical researchable questions is what we call 'operationalization', which has already been discussed in the context of the Science Cycle (chapter 2). This part of the research process is highlighted in figure 21.

In this chapter, we will guide you through the process of developing an adequate and manageable methodological framework. You have to ask yourself the following guiding questions during this step of the research process:

1 What (kind of) information is required in order to answer the research question?
2 What approach is the most appropriate for answering the research question?
3 Which methods are the most appropriate for producing the data needed?

Below we will elaborate more on these questions.

1   What (kind of) information is required in order to answer the research question?

The question you are trying to answer can take many forms. It can, for example, be an observational or experimental question, but might also be a question that leads to problem solving. The starting point can also be a prediction or a hypothesis instead of a question. In any case, you will have to unravel different features that are relevant with regard to the problem, prediction, or hypothesis in order to be able to answer or test it. Therefore, you first need to divide it into sub-questions. These sub-questions can be either disciplinary or interdisciplinary. For example, to what extent is aggressive behavior caused by a failure of self-control? And how is alcohol use modifying such self-control? Is behavioral self-control comparable to cognitive self-control?

Furthermore, your question and sub-questions contain concepts that you need to operationalize, and you therefore need to define exactly what you mean by these concepts. For example, when you are researching aggressive behavior, you should first define it and distinguish it from, for instance, assertive behavior. If you aim to focus on behavioral self-control, then you might need to operationalize how you aim to study this in practice and what standards you will be using. In other words, you are developing one or more ways for translating relevant concepts into researchable items (see also chapter 2). Since interdisciplinary research is often exploring new fields, existing methods are not always sufficient to operationalize your research question. That is why creativity is very important during this phase of the research project.

To operationalize your research question, it can be very useful, if not essential, to look into the possibilities of integrating the research approaches, methods, or techniques that are rooted in different disciplines. There are several possible techniques to integrate different approaches, methods, or techniques. Just as we saw in the previous chapter, you need to consider the type of change you need to make to existing methods and techniques in order to be able to find results with which you can answer your integrated research question. You may need to add an extra measuring technique, adjust a specific method, or connect different methods and techniques with each other (see figure 22).

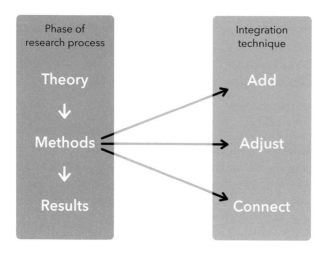

Figure 22   Possible integration techniques at the level of methodology

2   What approach is the most appropriate to answer the research question?
The way you translate theories and concepts into a useful operationalization depends on your approach. As we saw in chapter 1, there are different ways of thinking about knowledge and how knowledge should and can be gained. The approach you take can be positivistic and quantitative, or interpretative and qualitative, or, especially in the case of interdisciplinary research, a combination of both (i.e. a mixed methods approach). In many cases, it is only through a combination of approaches that one is able to get to a more complete understanding (see also methodological pluralism, as introduced in chapter 2). The approach you use also depends on the kind of question you ask. In the case of interdisciplinary research, it is often worthwhile considering using different approaches at the same time.

3   Which methods are the most appropriate to produce the data needed?
There are different ways to find an answer to this question, and the answer you find will depend, to some extent, on the operationalization you have chosen and the methods and techniques that you will use. For example, the results of a specific qualitative case study will differ from a quantitative comparative study into the same topic, but there will be some kind of correspondence between the two. An interdisciplinary goal would be to integrate these results irrespective of their methodological differences: probably the qualitative insights might help us to adjust our questionnaires and thus contribute to enhanced quantitative research.
To find out what the customary methods and techniques are in different disciplines, it is wise to return to your data management table (see figure 18). The table provides a brief overview of the articles you have read and analyzed so far, and you can learn from these articles how the key concepts have been operationalized in the different theoretical frameworks. You then have to decide with what adaptation or combination of these methodologies you can perform your own research.

Preferences for specific methods are common within disciplines. But if you perform research into a problem that crosses disciplinary boundaries, a combination of techniques often offers more accurate results. Furthermore, you might consider using your knowledge of and skills in a disciplinary method that is new to a particular problem.

It is perfectly possible that a technique used in discipline A cannot be used in the exact same way in discipline B. In that case, you might need to adjust the technique. Another possibility can be the adjustment of a specific theory and to use it as input for a data gathering technique in another field. In box 10 you will find examples of student projects where integration took place after methods or techniques were added, adjusted, or connected.

The choice of method, the practical limitations of methods, and the time allotted for your research may force you to reconsider your research question and adapt it to the research means. This is part of the iterative process that is inherent to interdisciplinary research. Adapting to the possibilities is challenging but unavoidable, so do not get discouraged too easily. Just be mindful that you might have to modify your research question because of practical limitations, and that this generally means you are moving forwards, not backwards!

Box 10
Examples of integration at the level of methods

Add a method
The influence of stress on human decision-making
Suppose you want to understand the influence of stress on human decision-making. Then you might consider using a device that measures the galvanic skin response under different test conditions (which conditions depends on the focus of your concrete research question) in order to get quantitative data on the physiological state of arousal, which can then be taken as a proxy for the stress level. But because this device cannot measure the subjective mental experience that accompanies the state of arousal, you might want to add a more qualitative type of measurement to differentiate between different mental states, like a short questionnaire (Maan, Cupido & van Moll, 2012).

Connecting methods
Measuring the weight of the dodo
In historical images of the dodo, this extinct bird is sometimes pictured as rather heavy, and sometimes as rather skinny. In addition, its weight was unknown. In their data management table, four students (van Dierendonck, van Egmond, ten Hagen & Kreuning, 2013) found that in

▼

many different methods were used to reconstruct the weight of the dodo. They past research, found differences in the reference species that was used (in other words: to which non-extinct bird species the dodo was compared), differences in the type of bones that were used as an indicator to determine overall weight of the animal, and differences in which part of the bone was measured. The students integrated elements of these research methods and their underlying assumptions into a new method, with which they were able to assess the dodo's weight more accurately.

Adding and connecting methods
Development of tumors
The development of tumors is usually the object of study for medical scientists. However, in their research project on tumor development, three students in psychobiology, medical biology, and econometrics learned that the behavior of tumor cells can also be studied from an economics perspective.

They used evolutionary game theory to create a model to describe and explain the behavior of tumor cells. Through the introduction of a way of studying that was new to the medical sciences, they found a new explanation for the development of tumors. This new information might offer new ways of fighting tumors by means of influencing the interaction between developing tumor cells (Dijkgraaf, Hooghiemstra & van der Spoel, 2009).

Adding and connecting theory and method
Volunteer tourism in Cuzco
During a research project on volunteer tourism in Cuzco, an interdisciplinary social scientist (Schram, 2012) wanted to learn more about how the different actors in volunteer tourism experience the power relations, and also how they evaluate the dependencies they experience. Interviewing relevant actors seems an appropriate research method. However, thoughts and feelings about power relations often appear to be part of a bigger narrative. Moreover, individuals are not always aware of their attitude toward it. It is therefore hard, if not impossible, to get relevant answers from actor interviews about these topics.

Positioning theory (from the field of social psychology) gives an explanation about how people define the 'self' in conversations. In his research project, Schram used the knowledge gained from positioning theory to improve the interview method: respondents were asked to write on Post-it notes the different groups of actors that, according to them, are involved in volunteer tourism in Cuzco. They were then asked to put the notes in two different orders:

▼

from least influence to most influence, and from independent to dependent. In this way, the positioning theory was used as a method in the domain of social interactions and it was thereby possible to gain insights into the way individuals perceive power relations.

Adjusting techniques for data analysis
Omega-3 fatty acid and heart rate variability
In order to find the impact of omega-3 fatty acid intake on heart rate variability (HRV) in men and women, two students with backgrounds in biomedical sciences and mathematics realized that first they had to look into the way HRV was being analyzed. They found the current technique to be outdated and they introduced a new technique for the analysis of HRV: the mathematical logarithm ApEn. This new technique and the use of an existing dataset allowed them to determine the influence of omega-3 fatty acid intake on the HRV in men and women with more accuracy. In this project, the analysis method of one discipline (mathematics) affected the data acquisition of another discipline (cardiology), as a slightly different data set was requested from cardiologists (Bekius & Elsenburg, 2010).

Step 7   Data collection and analysis

When you have selected a (disciplinary) method, you also commit to the standard (disciplinary) criteria and standards to collect and analyze data with that method. However, when you have translated or adjusted a method or technique, this may mean you have to reconsider your methods of data collection and analysis and possibly adjust them, without negatively affecting the validity, reliability, and accuracy of the method (see the Omega-3 fatty acid and heart rate variability example in Box 10).

A first step in data analysis is checking the raw data. Some of your data may simply not be useful or false (for example as a consequence of a mistake in an experiment). Suppose that you used survey questionnaires as a method for data collection and asked about the age of the participants. If somebody filled in '763 years old', you know this cannot be true and you have to adjust the otherwise skewed results.

In some cases you need to categorize, or code your data. There are different techniques for coding data and, as mentioned previously, the technique you choose depends on the kind of data you collected and the goal and approach of your research. If you use a quantitative approach, your data should be coded in a way that allows you to perform statistical analysis. For example, if you asked participants about work satisfaction and the possible answers to choose from were 'not satisfied', 'more or less satisfied' and 'very satisfied', you need to label these categories with different numbers before you can use them in statistical analyses. If you use a qualitative approach, you should also code your data. You need to think about the themes or variables you want to use to analyze and mark different parts of your data that correspond with that theme or variable, before you can interpret the data set.

It is possible and even advisable to use multiple techniques to analyze the same data. Integration of different data analysis techniques might actually improve the quality of your research project and the robustness of its outcomes.

After you have checked and coded the data, performed statistical analysis of different variables, and/or described the meaning of different themes within your data, it is time to connect different variables and themes. In order to do this, you need to explain how different themes and variables are related to each other. If you used both qualitative and quantitative analysis of the same data, you need to bring together the findings resulting from both analyses. You also need to think about the way you are going to present or visualize the data or findings. This can be done by means of graphs and/or tables, but there are numerous other ways. Note that in different disciplines, different ways to visualize the data are the norm. Especially when carrying out interdisciplinary research as a team, communication of the results is key, not only to the outside world, but also within the research team. Therefore, it is important to look for the optimal way of visualizing your data, in a way that is understandable across the involved disciplines. Eventually, this information should enable you to answer your sub-questions.

11 Discussion and conclusion(s)

Now that you have analyzed your data, it is time to discuss your results and reach a conclusion. You must first decide which technique to use to integrate your results. Once you have integrated them, your results will either verify or falsify the hypothesis (or hypotheses) you have been testing. To wrap up the story, it is helpful for the reader if you reiterate your research process by retracing and sharing your steps. Note that the order in which the discussion and conclusion(s) are presented in research papers differs from discipline to discipline and from journal to journal. In our model we place the discussion before the conclusion(s) (figure 23).

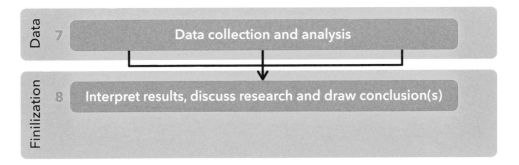

Figure 23   Steps 7 and 8 of the IIS model for interdisciplinary research

Considerations:
- Do the results confirm your hypothesis or expectations from your integrated theoretical framework?
- Does your interdisciplinary insight (or solution) shed new light on the insights obtained by each discipline separately?
- Spell out to your readers, who will often be disciplinary scientists – how specific disciplinary insights have been integrated into your interdisciplinary conclusion and, conversely, how this might have an impact on their future disciplinary research.
- What parts of your interdisciplinary research may be sensitive to criticism, and why?
- Based on your results, what research question would you want to pose next?

Step 8 Interpret results, discuss research & draw conclusion(s)

In chapter 6 we showed that integration can be conducted at multiple levels or at multiple locations in a complex system or mechanism. During this final step of the research process, it is often a matter of connecting results, rather than adding elements or adjusting them, although it is likely that you will end up combining all of them during the analysis (see box 11). Integration of results is usually necessary in the case of optimization problems. Furthermore, integration of results takes place when research leads to practical solutions or products. The conclusions of your research project are likely to raise new questions. Based on those new questions you can give recommendations for future research.

Creating a conceptual model can be a way to visualize and integrate your results (like the example on fisheries in box 4 on p. 47). With such a model, you are able to give an orderly representation of the system or problem you have researched. Consequently, you can uncover interactions between different aspects of the problem that are typically addressed by different disciplines

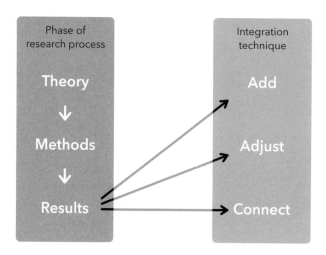

Figure 24   Possible integration techniques at the level of results

Example of integration at the level of results

Connect and optimize results

Finding the optimal location for the generation of sustainable energy in Mexico

A group of three students (van Dun, Muller & Boeke 2012) carried out a study on sustainable energy in Mexico. They found that given the amount of wave energy in the seas surrounding Mexico, the generation of offshore wave energy appears to be a promising technique. However, in order to generate and distribute energy properly, a stable political situation is essential. So, to give an answer to the question how wave energy can be best implemented in Mexico, both natural sciences (physics and earth science) and social sciences (political science) are necessary. They first analyzed in which regions of Mexico the most energy is used, and then mapped the degree of social and political stability in these regions. It turned out that the optimal location in terms of energy yield did not match the optimal location with regards to political stability. So, it ultimately came down to optimization between the regions with the highest amount of wave energy and the most stable political situation (van Dun et al., 2012).

At the beginning of the research project, you started with a problem, which you then narrowed down into a research question and sub-questions. Subsequently, you chose methods to answer your main question and sub-questions. In this process of specifying the problem, you likely have made several choices, which may have forced you to reconsider choices you made in previous steps. In order to formulate a well-considered discussion, you need to reflect on all the choices you made throughout the project that might have influenced the results.

But the first task at hand is to answer your research question. The following questions form a guideline that may help you structure the discussion/conclusions chapter.

- Why did you need an interdisciplinary perspective – i.e. what were likely shortcomings of disciplinary perspectives?
- What was your research question?
- From the perspective of the integrated, interdisciplinary theoretical framework that you have prepared, what answer(s) did you expect?
- What results did you find?
- How do you interpret these results in the context of your theoretical framework?
- What repercussions could your research and conclusion have for those disciplinary perspectives involved in your study?
- What advice for further disciplinary studies could you draw from this?

Even if the results completely confirm your hypothesis, it is always possible to discuss the choices and interpretations you made during the research process. Also, your results are often supported by previous research, but there are likely results that do not necessarily warrant as conclusions. Do not ignore those alternative explanations, but give them a place in your discussion. In other words, discuss your results in the context of the total coverage of the literature. Also, articulate and reflect upon the limitations of your study's methods – and suggest possible follow-up studies. When discussing your study, you could, for example, answer the following questions:

- Does your method/or do your methods contain elements that leave room for alternative explanations?
- Are there alternative points of view from which your results could be interpreted in a different way?

Up to this point, your conclusion and discussion chapter is not really very different from one you would find in a disciplinary paper, except that the information is provided by multiple academic disciplines. However, there is more to reflect upon: the interdisciplinary research process you followed and the surplus value of your interdisciplinary approach.

- Did the interdisciplinary research process lead to unexpected insights? If so, where did they occur?
- Were these insights into the main research question, or tangential to your line of inquiry?
- Were there steps specified in the model on interdisciplinary research provided by this manual that did not fit the project well? If so, how did you adjust the process?
- Overall, what did you learn about the interdisciplinary process?
- Do your interdisciplinary insights shed new light on the individual insights from each discipline? Or can your insights be criticized for lacking depth or being too reductionist?
- Has your analysis perhaps unearthed some important issues that deserve more attention?
- Which gaps in knowledge still exist and, moreover, which gaps in knowledge have surfaced as a result of the insights provided by your research?
- What opportunities do you see for new research (directions)?

You may also include tips for improvement as you consider the approach you have chosen, as well as making suggestions for future research as you draw your paper to a close.

You have now taken all the steps that eventually led to an interdisciplinary answer to your integrated research question. You have brought together different disciplinary insights and integrated them in order to get a more complete and inclusive understanding of the complex problem you have researched. It is now time to write a report on your interdisciplinary research. In this report, it is also important to systematically reflect on your research, which poses new questions. Note that this is more complex in the case of interdisciplinary science, as you not only address future interdisciplinary research, but also inspire disciplinary science that relates to your research topic. Therefore, it is important to be aware of the fact that you are not targeting a specific audience, but rather appeal to a diverse audience consisting of both disciplinary and interdisciplinary academics. It is your task to give suggestions for both future disciplinary research as well as interdisciplinary research. So, this is where you also point out what the relevance of this particular interdisciplinary research project is for 'normal science'.

Part 3
Interdisciplinary research in practice

Now that you have read parts 1 and 2, you have an idea about the origins of and drivers towards interdisciplinary research, as well as what it entails. You have read what it takes to engage in interdisciplinary research and what the specific steps are that an interdisciplinary researcher needs to take. In this third part, we show how interdisciplinary research is conducted in practice. We will illustrate this with a step-by-step description of an interdisciplinary students' research project (chapter 12). In addition, we interviewed four interdisciplinary academics about their careers, giving you an idea of what the life of an interdisciplinarian might look like (chapter 13).

12 Interdisciplinary research example: fogponics

A group of five bachelor students did their interdisciplinary capstone research project on fogponics, a promising and innovative way to grow crops (Bakker, van der Linden, Steenbrink, Stuut & Veldhuyzen van Zanten, 2014). In this chapter, their interdisciplinary research process is described in accordance with our interdisciplinary research model, step by step.

Step 1   Identify problem or topic

The five students were interested in sustainable agriculture and after some brainstorming and an initial literature search, they came up with an innovative way of growing crops sustainably.

Agriculture is a mostly unsustainable form of land use, because its energy and water consumption, and pollution (from fertilizers, pesticides, herbicides, etc.) are exceeding certain limits. Moreover, the global human population will continue to grow in the coming decades, further pushing the demand for food production. New, efficient and sustainable forms of agriculture have to be developed in order to cope with these challenges. Vertical farming (agriculture on vertically inclined surface such as within a skyscraper) might contribute to a solution to the problems related to conventional agriculture, or, more specifically greenhouse production. Fogponics, as will be explained later on, might be a suitable and sustainable way to grow crops in a vertical farming setting.

This research will focus on the situation in the Netherlands, as a lot of information on the Dutch greenhouse sector is available. A further demarcation is the focus on a specific crop, tomatoes, which will be further explained under Step 3.

Relevant disciplines

In this case, the relevant disciplines were partly determined by the disciplines that the group of students had previously chosen. Other disciplines could have been relevant with regards to this topic, although the final research question was defined in such a way that the following contributing disciplines were sufficient for answering it:

- Biology: plants,
- Chemistry: nutrients,
- Artificial Intelligence: system operating,
- Mathematics: extrapolating calculations,
- Economics: costs.

Dominant perspectives (with regard to the problem and the contemplated solution)

- Biology: agriculture is mostly unsustainable as pollution is exceeding certain limits. Fogponics might contribute to a more sustainable form of agriculture. Biology can shed light on the physiological aspects on the growing of crops within a fogponics context.
- Chemistry: agriculture is mostly unsustainable as it requires significant energy inputs but fossil fuels become increasingly scarce. In order for fogponics to be a sustainable alternative, chemistry is needed to make the use of nutrients and water as efficiently as possible.
- Artificial Intelligence (AI): AI focuses on 'intelligent' systems. In this case, AI can help to design a fogponics system that operates autonomously. Furthermore, it can help to optimize this system when implemented on a larger scale.
- Mathematics: n/a.
- Economics: the world population will have outgrown the maximum production of the current agriculture system by 2050. Hence, from an economic perspective, our current system will not be sustainable or cost-efficient in the long term. Economics can help to assess the cost-efficiency of fogponics on a larger scale.

Step 2   Formulate preliminary research question

While integrating the relevant perspectives of their respective disciplines, the team of students formulated the following research question: To what extent can fogponics contribute to sustainable agriculture?

Relevant theories, concepts, and assumptions

Looking for relevant contributions from their respective disciplines to answer the main research question, the students subsequently formulated potential disciplinary distributions. Biology, they contended, can shed light on the physiological aspects of crops. Furthermore, biology can help to select the optimal crop species for an experimental fogponics setting. Chemistry is relevant for measuring and analyzing nutrients used by the plants. By using mathematical models, an extrapolation can be made from the experimental level to the national level. Based on economic insights, finally, a comparison can be made between the costs of the use of water and nutrients in fogponics systems and in current greenhouses.

Step 3   Develop theoretical framework

In rocky habitats close to waterfalls, plants grow with roots that 'hang' in the fog generated by the falling water. This observation inspired plant biologists to develop aeroponics systems (systems where 'hanging' roots are sprinkled with water) to study root functioning. Aeroponics systems were subsequently developed into a setup where water is provided in the form of fog, the so-called 'fogponics system'. This research project is inspired by such a fogponics system, because it might also be used in a commercial crop production setting.

Tomatoes (*Solanum lycopersicum*) are the world's second largest crop in terms of production. Additionally, tomatoes are an important export product for the

Netherlands, currently the largest tomato-exporting country in the world. These are two arguments to use tomatoes as a model organism in the fogponics system. Chemistry can help measure the amount of nutrients used by the plant. This can be analyzed by means of high-performance liquid chromatography (HPLC), a method to identify and quantify the components of a mixture. There is a high variance in the amount of cations (positively charged ions) and a low variance in the amount of anions (negatively charged ions) in the nutrient water. Using a cation-exchange HPLC, one can measure the amount of cations in the liquid. These cations represent nutrients; thus, one is able to measure the amount of nutrients.

To compare fogponics with current greenhouse agriculture in terms of nutrient and water use, it is essential to make an assessment of the costs, production capacity, and use of resources (i.e. nutrients and water) of fogponics in the long term. This can be done using the relationship between plant growth and water and nutrient use. Plant growth can be simulated by means of a mathematical growth model.

To make a fogponics system as efficient as possible, to optimize it, artificial intelligence (AI) can provide useful tools. AI can develop an expert system to regulate circulation and nutrient concentrations of the water in a fogponics system. Such a system is semi-autonomous and possesses the ability to learn, thereby improving efficiency. Sustainability and efficiency have to go hand in hand to be consistent with the main research question in this project.

The World Commission on Environment and Development (1987) defined sustainable development as "development which meets the needs of the present without compromising the ability of future generations to meet their own needs." In this research, sustainability is defined as an interdisciplinary concept, encompassing both environmental and economic stakes or needs.

Step 4 Finalize research question

The final question is somewhat different from the preliminary research question, as the students had now decided under what specific conditions they would experiment with fogponics. As a result, the final clause was changed and specified, leading to the question: To what extent can fogponics contribute to a more sustainable form of greenhouse cultivation? As explained earlier, this was done by means of a case study on greenhouse production of tomatoes in the Netherlands.

Step 5 Formulate sub-questions

Given the limitations of a student project and the majors involved, the students had to limit and specify their sub-questions too. They decided to focus on nutrient and water use, as they are highly relevant for any agricultural project's sustainability. As a result, the research question is sub-divided into two sub-questions:

- Is fogponics a good alternative in terms of efficient nutrient use to conventional greenhouse agriculture?
- Is fogponics a good alternative in terms of efficient water use to conventional greenhouse agriculture?

In this research project, a combination of both empirical and theoretical research was used, in which different disciplines played key roles. This is illustrated in figure 25. The empirical data on plant growth in a fogponics system were collected using an experimental setting, which involved the disciplines of (plant) biology and chemistry. On the other hand, theoretical research was done, which consisted of a study on the economics of tomato greenhouse cultivation and another study on how to optimize the fogponics system (using knowledge from AI). The data from the experiment were used as input for the mathematical extrapolation, on the basis of which the theoretical part of this research was carried out. As you can see, this is an integration of methods, making the research truly interdisciplinary.

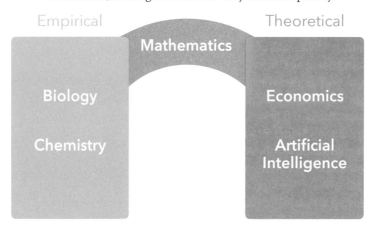

Figure 25   Schematic representation of the relation between the disciplines contributing to the research (Bakker et al., 2014)

During the experiment, daily samples of the water were taken and nutrient concentrations were measured with HPLC. Deficits in nutrient concentrations were replenished. Due to the limited duration of the project, the tomato plants did not reach maturity during the course of the experiment. To be able to assess the amount of water and nutrients needed by full-grown plants, the total length of all stems of the tomato plants were measured and used to create a growth curve (figure 27). This growth curve formed the basis for an extrapolation of water and nutrient use. Then, the students calculated the hypothetical water and nutrient use of the whole Dutch tomato greenhouse sector based on the fogponics method. Subsequently, this was compared to economic data on conventional greenhouse cultivation (water use, nutrient use, and costs). This was largely done on the basis of literature research.

Step 7 Data collection and analysis

In order to give an answer to the main research question – to what extent can fogponics contribute to a more sustainable form of greenhouse cultivation? – plant measurements had to be extrapolated to potential greenhouse tomato yields on the national level.

Plant growth was measured during approximately 25 days. The results of the plant growth measurements were extrapolated using an S-growth curve, because this one best describes growth of tomato plants. An extrapolated graph was created by means of a logistic growth function (see figure 27). Number of days is displayed on the x-axis and total plant length (including all stems) is displayed on the y-axis. Using a logistic growth function, the students were able to determine the maximum plant length the tomato plants would reach in the fogponics setting is about 600 cm.

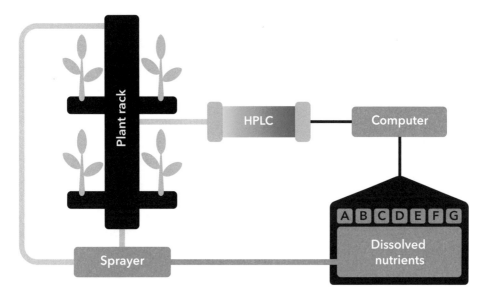

Figure 26   Experimental fogponics system (Bakker et al., 2014)

Subsequently, the amount of nutrients and water needed for full-grown plants was calculated. These amounts were compared to those needed in the current greenhouse tomato sector in the Netherlands. The students found that the fogponics system needs approximately 30% of the water and just 14% of the nutrients used in conventional greenhouse cultivation of tomatoes. This, in turn, leads to a yearly reduction of costs of around € 7,000,000 in the Netherlands.

Discussion

The results confirm the hypothesis that fogponics can contribute to sustainable agriculture, both in terms of environmental and economic needs. These promising results, together with the interdisciplinary insight in the valuable combination of fogponics with commercial agriculture, create possibilities for new developments in sustainable agriculture.

This interdisciplinary research, in turn, raises several new (disciplinary) research questions. For example, in this project, sustainability was demarcated to water and nutrient use and costs. However, there are other aspects of sustainability that were not taken into account. Future research focusing on, among others, energy consumption, resource use, and waste production will lead to a more complete picture of the sustainability of fogponics.

The students realized that a few aspects might have undesirably influenced the results of the research. First, the tubes in which the tomato plants were placed were not completely closed. Consequently, leakage of fog occurred. It is unclear how much water and nutrients leaked away from the system. Moreover, potential negative effects of a completely closed system on plant growth cannot be ruled out.

Second, due to the limitations of the research project, it was necessary to extrapolate the data derived from a small, unreplicated experiment. Therefore, the experiment should be repeated and the experiment time extended so that tomato plants can produce their entire yield.

Third, several assumptions were made concerning the production of tomato plants. These assumptions were partly based on literature and interviews with experts. Nonetheless, these numbers (growth rate means, etc.) might not correspond exactly with reality, as different, unidentified factors may also influence the results.

Conclusion

Compared to conventional greenhouse agriculture, fogponics is more efficient in terms of water use. Additionally, fogponics is also more efficient than conventional agriculture in terms of nutrient use. Consequently, fogponics has the potential to significantly reduce costs of Dutch tomato production: costs can be reduced by approximately 85%. The conclusion can be drawn that fogponics is indeed more sustainable – both in terms of ecology and economics – than conventional greenhouse agriculture.

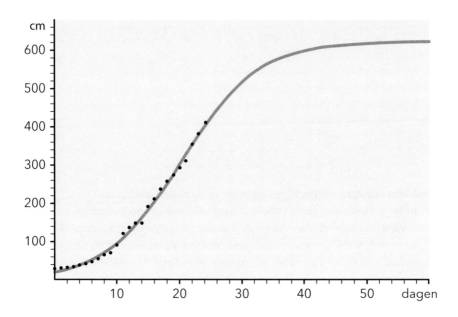

Figure 27 Extrapolated growth curve of tomato plants (Bakker et al., 2014)

Integration of insights can also yield new interventions like a new technology. In this case, the students built an experimental fogponics system geared to their insights and research question, using plastic pipework. Before entering the system, nutrients are added to distilled water in the necessary quantities. The water is subsequently led through the system to the dispenser. This dispenser uses ultrasonic oscillations to turn the water into fog, which is led through the tubes in which the roots of the tomato plants are hanging, so they can take up the nutrients. The remaining fog condenses and returns to the dispenser to ensure continuous circulation.

13 Interdisciplinary careers

In the previous chapters we discussed what interdisciplinary research entails, when it can be applied, and why it should be applied. We have seen throughout that interdisciplinary research is – more so than disciplinary research – by its very nature determined by the particular research questions and context. This also affects the background, careers and activities of interdisciplinarians themselves. Indeed, by looking at the biographies and statements of a few interdisciplinarians you may recognize this context dependence as well as the pluralism in terms of scientific contents and methods that are challenging and inspiring them.

The first example represents the relatively large group of interdisciplinarians with a background in two different disciplines, allowing them to critically consider the questions, contents, and methods of each discipline in itself and the assumptions that are underlying them.

"One has to find a language that is understandable to all the groups you acquired information from"

Prof. dr. Trudy Dehue
Professor at the University of Groningen

Trudy Dehue was first trained as a psychologist and then as a philosopher of science at the University of Groningen. In her transdisciplinary and interdisciplinary research, she focuses on psychology and psychiatry. She has written three books, *Changing the Rules*, *De Depressie-epidemie* (The Depression Epidemic), and *Betere Mensen* (Better People).

How did I get involved in interdisciplinary research? I guess it was my curiosity and a deep awareness that people always argue from particular perspectives. Historically speaking, the explanation might be that my parents hardly ever agreed on anything. My mother's story about an event was usually completely different from my father's version of the same event and as a child I soon discovered they were both right in a way.

When I was in my twenties, I got my first job, which was at a children's psychiatric clinic. There, the problems of a child, his or her family, and the larger context were viewed from all kinds of perspectives. This job made me want to understand more about psychological issues. Hence, I went to the university and graduated in psychology and philosophy. I was always trying to compare and, if possible, combine divergent points of view. It is like a habit for me to look for other perspectives, try to weigh them and make a coherent new story out of them.

My main motivation to study psychological subjects in an interdisciplinary fashion is that I am interested in real life issues and not so much in problems generated by scientific paradigms. That is, I am not only interested in comparing views and data stemming from academics such as philosophers, psychologists, sociologists, historians, or neuroscientists, but also in including views of journalists, teachers, patients, or parents and children. The idea of transdisciplinarity is that non-academics can generate valuable knowledge as well. For instance, politicians can be interesting too. Another example: I also took the knowledge of illegal drug users into account when I studied the subject of drug abuse.

My interest in drug use or abuse was triggered when I started to analyze the inherent assumptions of the so-called 'golden standard' of scientific proof, the randomized controlled experiment or RCT. An RCT is a kind of experiment commonly used for testing the efficacy of a medical treatment or any other kind of intervention in humans or animals. One compares randomly composed experimental groups and control groups that respectively receive and do not receive the treatment under scrutiny.

Originally, my main example was the scientific experiment with providing free heroin for heroin abusers that ran in the late twentieth century in the Netherlands. To me that topic was interdisciplinary from the very start. In my writings about it, I applied views from sociology and philosophy of science. Using a cultural anthropological perspective, I also explored what it means to be a heroin user and I studied knowledge about drug legislation. This project was truly transdisciplinary as well. I studied debates in parliament about the heroin experiment and talked to heroin users or their representatives.

At present, the challenges for interdisciplinary and transdisciplinary research are immense, because academics are used to specializing and are accustomed to their own frameworks with their own assumptions, language, and rules. Even in the psychology building where I work it is hard for people to understand one another, because, for instance, social, clinical and theoretical psychologists work in quite divergent research traditions. When writing an interdisciplinary book or article one has to find a language that is neutral enough to be understandable to all the groups you acquired your information from.

My tip for aspiring interdisciplinary researchers would be: be interested and involved, read and study, learn from all kinds of people and, most importantly, subsequently think for yourself. In addition, don't worry too much about traditional boundaries because these are gradually losing their supremacy.

Do many interdisciplinarians have backgrounds in more than just a single discipline? Some disciplines are in themselves rather interdisciplinary, as is the case with the background of our next example: cultural psychology. This (sub-) discipline focuses on the impact of cultural context on the cognition and behavior of subjects and integrates insights from several disciplines – ranging from genetics to cultural anthropology. Over time, an interdisciplinary field or inter-discipline like cultural psychology can become established as such, which suggests that there is already some consensus on the questions, contents, methods and the like within the community of cultural psychologists. Nonetheless, as the field of cultural psychology still attracts collaborators from different and new disciplines, researchers need to adapt to the specific context and group within which they conduct their research. As this requires them to articulate and exchange their ideas on the questions, contents and methods that matter to them, this also asks for a lot of trust between them: trust in the sense of respect for each other and trust in the sense of relying upon the expertise of each other.

"A key factor in doing interdisciplinary research is trust"

Prof. dr. Tom ter Bogt
director of the bachelor Interdisciplinary Social Sciences
(Algemene Sociale Wetenschappen) at Utrecht University

As a student in cultural psychology I was trained in interdisciplinarity. A basic principle of cultural psychology is that genes, personality, or the brain alone cannot explain behavior of individuals, simply because their (cultural) environment poses a big influence as well as constraints. You have to add a cultural context, which also influences cognition, emotions, and behavior. This interdisciplinary idea really appealed to me, and as a student I learned to mix classic, biological theories about genes and brains with psychological theories on personality and contextual theories from sociology and anthropology.
Currently, I am employed as a professor in youth culture at Utrecht University. Here, I study the effects of cultural contexts on behavior as well. For example, I recently published an article on drug use. One fundamental explanation in psychology is that adolescents who use drugs, score higher on the trait sensation seeking. However, it is unlikely that someone who scores high on this trait would have used drugs in the Netherlands in the 1950s, simply because drugs were not available in large numbers. When cannabis and other drugs were introduced in larger numbers in the 1960s, the context suddenly changed. Sensation seekers were drawn toward these drugs.
In the article, I also showed that there was another cultural factor that played a

role in drug use. In the 60s, mainly highly educated adolescents ('hippies' for example) used drugs, but this has shifted over the years toward adolescents with a lower socio-economic status. I found a similar pattern across nations: in earlier days drugs were mainly used in rich European countries, but nowadays drugs are predominantly used in poor countries, for instance in Eastern Europe. So it turned out that a constellation of factors, such as personality and environment, influences drug use by adolescents. And moreover, these factors are not stable. Environments, for instance, are culturally variant. This constellation of moving factors is a part of the explanation why people use drugs.

I mainly draw my inspiration for research topics from discussions with researchers from other disciplinary backgrounds. As a member of the risk-behavior group of Health Behavior in School-aged Children (HBSC), an international organization of researchers on health-related problems, I talk to researchers from various disciplinary backgrounds, such as psychology, sociology, and medicine. We also collaborate in research projects. One researcher usually takes the lead and poses a topic or a hypothesis he or she wants to study, which usually results in a team of four or five researchers from other disciplines who are also interested in the topic. Because I am working with people from various disciplinary backgrounds, I develop a sense for different aspects of a problem. For example, I wasn't interested in policies a bit, until a researcher with a background in policy sciences asked me: "I think the liberal law considering drug use in the Netherlands is quite interesting. How about investigating whether this policy has an effect on cannabis consumption and compare this to alcohol use?" I had missed that factor in my previous studies and I thoroughly enjoyed doing this research, despite my initial reservations about policy sciences.

A key factor in doing interdisciplinary research is trust. You have to form coalitions with experts in fields that you do not fully understand sometimes. If you want to add insights from neuroscience, for example, you have to form a coalition with an expert from that field to check whether the neuroscientific theories are correctly incorporated in your model. You have to trust the expert. Also, it has to be someone you can work with. It is through discussions with these other experts that you eventually develop a model; you integrate the different perspectives from the disciplinary experts into one interdisciplinary perspective. Therefore, I only work together with people that inspire me, or researchers who think I have an interesting story to tell.

Some interdisciplinary researchers have a background in two different disciplines, some have a background in a discipline that is already established as an interdisciplinary discipline – as is the case with cultural psychology – while still others have a background in an interdiscipline that is relatively new. In that case, there is not yet much consensus on the questions, contents and methods that are central to the field. This seems to be the case with 'transition science', which draws from a wide range of disciplines. Moreover, as a transition usually affect non-academic stakeholders – like clients, patients, citizens – such trans-disciplinary research projects must also involve these groups along the way. The openness and trust that interdisciplinarians have to employ in their work is needed even more in these cases. The example below confirms nicely what we have argued above: interdisciplinary research does not replace disciplinary research, as the latter is still needed in most interdisciplinary research projects. Yet, embedding disciplinary research in such projects does challenge disciplinary scholars to adjust and expand their way of going about in their research in all phases.

"The transition framework serves as a shared pair of glasses, or a method to communicate across disciplinary boundaries"

Dr. Derk A. Loorbach
director of the Dutch Research Institute for Transitions, DRIFT

Derk Loorbach studied Culture and Science Studies at Maastricht University, with a specialization in European studies.

It was a relatively new program at the time and the main mode of education was problem-based learning (PBL). Students therefore automatically developed an interdisciplinary mindset, because the problem – not the disciplinary theoretical background – was the starting point of any research project.
After that, I started working at the International Centre for Integrative Studies (ICIS) in Maastricht. At this institute, research focuses on topics such as human health, water, tourism, mobility, and biodiversity, making use of participatory methods, scenario analysis, transition management, and modeling techniques. This is where I met Jan Rotmans, one of the pioneers in transition science.
The concept of transitions was something I found very appealing. At the time, a lot of technological transitions had been described, but the idea of societal transitions in a sustainable direction was new. I believe that our current society is unsustainable and bound to break out of its locked-in state. But how can we influence such a transition, or maybe even accelerate it? The concept of transition is a mental construction that is understandable for a lot of different people, a means of communication across different perspectives and values that helps to generate shared insights and thereby stimulates us to engage in collaborative research projects. The concept can be applied in both a transdisciplinary context, in collaboration with stakeholders, and in an interdisciplinary context, where the focus lies on complex societal systems. Soon, we initiated a national research program, in which all kinds of different academic fields were involved, ranging from history, innovation sciences, sociology, psychology, public administration, business administration, economics, political science, and philosophy to theoretical

physics. And soon after that, the Dutch Research Institute for Transitions (DRIFT) was founded at Erasmus University Rotterdam.

At DRIFT we collaborate closely with the Stockholm Resilience Centre, which focuses mostly on ecology. This is an interesting collaboration, as both institutes focus on transitions, albeit in slightly different ways. From an ecological point of view, one wants to prevent a (socio-) ecological system from undergoing a 'negative transition', or especially a collapse. But at the same time, a societal transition is needed in order to prevent such a collapse. I am director at DRIFT now and, as such, my mission is to expand our research practices, but also to do my own 'transition experiment' to innovate the science system, which I think is still largely discipline-based, with little or no interaction across disciplinary lines.

In our research projects, we always go from trans- to inter- to multidisciplinarity. We start by defining the research focus in a transdisciplinary context, because we need societal input to formulate the main question as accurately and appropriately as possible. We then shift to an interdisciplinary approach, further researching and analyzing the problem. And then we often come to underlying questions that need to be addressed from a disciplinary perspective. After that, we return to the transdisciplinary level. The other way around – starting with disciplines – doesn't work, because there is no incentive for shared insights. In our projects, it's always a combination of those different modes, and one can see a recurring cyclic process in our research.

For example, in a project on sustainable cities and ecosystem services, we've got people who are concerned with the practical questions, looking at the dynamics of a city and the role of ecosystems. At the same time, other researchers ask themselves interdisciplinary questions about the city: What is the objective for a city? Which patterns, and which barriers can we identify? And then we have the modelers and planners who are working in a more disciplinary fashion. Eventually, we end up at the transdisciplinary level again.

The starting point of many, if not all of our research projects is a complex problem. And in practice, complexity means that you need more disciplines and perspectives to understand what you're talking about. But there has to be a shared interest, or a sense of urgency. In our case, the transition framework serves as a shared pair of glasses, or a method to communicate across disciplinary boundaries, a "boundary object" as we like to call it, or an integration method. It's a kind of semi-neutral territory needed to get beyond individual perspectives. In the academic world, we call those perspectives "disciplines" and in society "world views".

It's hard to pinpoint when and where interdisciplinary integration happens, since it's a normal condition for us. I don't recognize when it happens exactly; I'd only recognize it if it didn't happen. And that never happens in practice, because it's the core of our work. But for me it's a mode of research that differs from multidisciplinarity. That's when you cut a problem into pieces beforehand and then you park those pieces at different research groups, only to put them in one report in the end, without any exchange of knowledge or insights.

In my opinion, when there is exchange on the subject of a shared question, you may speak about interdisciplinarity. Broadly speaking, I think there are three key *moments in this process, although they are not always easy to identify and more often form a continuous process. The first moment is the initial contact between researchers about something they have in common. The second is when shared insights are generated, when they discover complementarities in their knowledge. The third moment is when this leads to a new in-depth insight, which is of value for their own disciplines as well. And as a consequence, connections between disciplines are established.*

One of the main drivers of interdisciplinary and transdisciplinary research is complexity, as we argued in the beginning of this handbook of interdisciplinary research. The complexity of nature and society and the complexity of developing solutions to some of the big issues we are currently facing – climate change, globalization, economic crisis – requires the insights and expertise of scientists from different disciplines and interdisciplines. In addition, these scientists need to be open to communicate with colleagues from other disciplines and with stakeholders from outside academia who have an interest in the issues at stake. A further characteristic of these complex and real-world projects is the fact that they often allow for more than just a single solution, which requires all those involved to navigate the complex trade-offs that exist between these solutions. As much as inter- and transdisciplinarians are required to be flexible in developing and conducting their research, they must also be flexible in terms of developing the tools to evaluate the results of it and perhaps implement them in a certain situation. The example below describes how developing several scenarios might be useful in facilitating such evaluation and the decision-making that ensues from it – scenario thinking being just one of the tools that might be used in such cases. When working with stakeholders, it is important for scientists to realize that they might not all be equally prepared or capable of participating in an activity like scenario thinking. Indeed, even at the final stage of a project, when only a suitable method for evaluation and implementation of its results is needed, researchers are required to be flexible and open.

"Scenario thinking enables you to get a perspective on multiple futures"

Dr. Joost Vervoort
scenario developer at Climate Change Agriculture and Food Security, Oxford University

Joost Vervoort holds a BSc in Biology and an MSc in Natural Resources Management from Utrecht University, and a PhD in Production Ecology and Resource Conservation from Wageningen University and Research Centre. The emphasis of his PhD project was on participatory scenario development to elicit stakeholder perspectives on socio-ecological systems change. Scenario research focuses on multiple plausible futures. On the basis of scenarios representing different futures, more adequate policies can be developed. As a consequence of the stakeholder participation, the research also involved social sciences such as political science and anthropology.

After his PhD, Vervoort got a position at Oxford University as a postdoctoral researcher at the Climate Change, Agriculture and Food Security (CCAFS) project. CCAFS focuses on the nexus between climate change, agriculture, and food security in the developing world. The main fields involved are climatology, environmental sciences (ecology, earth sciences), and agricultural science, which are interdisciplinary and multidisciplinary fields in themselves. Governance, food security (which involves access to food, food prices, and division of food), and political context are also of great importance. So, both the natural and social sciences are essential to CCAFS research, employing scenarios as a tool. Scenario thinking originated in the corporate world. Companies such as Royal Dutch Shell started with strategic scenario planning in the 1970s. It enabled them to anticipate the oil crisis and, as a result, by the end of the 1970s, Shell was one of the world's biggest oil concerns. It is because of these success stories that scenario analysis subsequently gained ground in the academic world.

Vervoort supports the use of this method:

Scenario thinking enables you to get a perspective on multiple futures. After all, the future is uncertain. The starting point is the fundamental complexity of the world we're living in. We ask ourselves 'What if a sudden change occurs?' instead of 'What is going to happen?' To be able to answer that question, different perspectives – both disciplinary and sectoral – are important. Our research involves socioeconomic, political, and biophysical aspects, and they are experienced differently in different sectors. We try to articulate them by means of scenarios, in participation with actors in the field such as local politicians, farmers, etc. It's interesting to see how scenarios are able to integrate knowledge. Scenarios are narratives, or stories. And those stories integrate knowledge by describing how different drivers – socioeconomic, political, biophysical – interact. Scenarios integrate disciplinary insights in a natural way. They thereby capture complexity.

The above four examples capture quite different academic biographies and descriptions of ongoing interdisciplinary projects. They should demonstrate that there is not a single trajectory that brings you to the challenging and fascinating domain of interdisciplinarity. On the contrary, a wide variety of such trajectories is possible, depending upon many contingencies but also upon your own background, interests, and capabilities. Perhaps more than in the case of a disciplinary trajectory you should take the time to articulate and reflect upon them – by yourself and in conversation with your peers and mentors. This, in combination with the experience of doing interdisciplinary research that you have gathered with the assistance of this handbook, will hopefully help you to proceed with a trajectory that suits you well.

Further reading

Now that you have experienced the interdisciplinary research process, you probably want to find out more about interdisciplinary research in the academic world. Interdisciplinary research can be found in many different forms and places; the following books and organizations are good places to start.

I   Books on interdisciplinary research

Interdisciplinary Research: Process and Theory
Allen Repko, Sage, 2012 (2nd edition)
This book is written for advanced undergraduate and graduate students and covers interdisciplinary research methods. It neatly describes how to achieve, produce, and express integration. This book can be very useful when writing an interdisciplinary research paper.

Introduction to Interdisciplinary Studies
Allen Repko, Rick Szostak, Michelle Phillips Buchberger, Sage, 2013
This book is an introduction to the principles of interdisciplinary studies. It can be very helpful when working with topics, problems, or themes that span multiple disciplines.

Case Studies in Interdisciplinary Research
Allen Repko, William Newell, Rick Szostak, Sage (eds.), 2011
These case studies, written by leading researchers in interdisciplinary research, show how to apply the interdisciplinary research process to a variety of problems.

Interdisciplinary Research Journeys
Catherine Lyall, Ann Bruce, Joyce Tait, Laura Meagher, FT Press, 2011
This book provides a practical guide for researchers and research managers who are seeking to develop interdisciplinary research strategies at a personal, institutional, and multi-institutional level.

Methods for Transdisciplinary Research
Matthias Bergmann, Thomas Jahn, Tobias Knobloch, Wolfgang Krohn, Christian
Pohl, Engelbert Schramm (eds.), Campus Verlag GmbH, 2013
This book provides scholars with a model for conceptualizing and executing
transdisciplinary research, while offering a systematic description of methods for
knowledge integration that can be applied to any field of research.

Enhancing Communication & Collaboration in Interdisciplinary Research
Michael O'Rourke, Stephen Crowley, Sanford Eigenbrode, Jeffrey Wulfhorst, Sage
(eds.), 2013
The book contains theoretical perspectives, case studies, communication tools,
and institutional perspectives of interdisciplinary research.

The Oxford Handbook of Interdisciplinarity
Robert Frodeman, Julie Thompson Klein, Carl Mitcham (eds.), OUP, 2012
This handbook provides a synoptic overview of the current state of interdisciplinary
research, education, administration, management, and problem-solving
knowledge that spans the disciplines and interdisciplinary fields, and crosses the
space between the academic community and society at large.

Facilitating Interdisciplinary Research
National Academy of Sciences, 2004
The report identifies steps that researchers, teachers, students, institutions,
funding organizations, and disciplinary societies can take to more effectively
conduct, facilitate, and evaluate interdisciplinary research programs and projects.
Throughout the report, key concepts are illustrated with case studies and results of
the committee's surveys of individual researchers and university provosts.

Interdisciplinarity: Essays from the Literature
William Newell (ed.) New York: College Entrance Examination Board, 1998
This is an interesting collection of essays on various aspects of interdisciplinarity,
ranging from administration to interdisciplinarity in different scientific domains.

Interdisciplinary Research: Case Studies from Health and Social Science
Frank Kessel,, Patricia Rosenfiel & Norman Anderson (eds.), OUP, 2008
Although the case studies in this volume all stem from health and social sciences,
their extensive analysis is illuminating for students from other fields as well.

II   Interdisciplinary organizations

The Association of Interdisciplinary Studies (AIS)
The AIS is the main interdisciplinary professional organization founded in 1979 to promote the interchange of ideas among scholars and administrators in all of the arts and sciences regarding interdisciplinarity and integration. The AIS journal Issues in Interdisciplinary Studies (formerly, Issues in Integrative Studies) publishes peer reviewed articles on a wide range of interdisciplinary topics, research, education and policy. (Editor and co-author Keestra is currently President of AIS.) http://www.oakland.edu/ais

Center for Interdisciplinary Research (ZiF)
ZiF was established in 1968 at the new Bielefeld University. It houses and funds interdisciplinary research projects in the natural sciences, humanities, and social sciences. http://www.uni-bielefeld.de/ZIF/

International Network for Interdisciplinarity & Transdisciplinarity (INIT)
INIT seeks to provide an international platform for the discussion and promotion of interdisciplinary and transdisciplinary research, teaching, and policy. INIT will inventory existing understandings, facilitate and enhance communication, and stimulate new research. http://www.inidtd.org/

Td-net
Td-net is a network initiated by the Swiss academy of sciences and advances the mutual learning between interdisciplinary and transdisciplinary researchers and lecturers across thematic fields, languages, and countries, thereby supporting community building. http://www.transdisciplinarity.ch

The Human Frontier Science Program (HFSP)
The HFSP is an international program of research support, funding frontier research on the complex mechanisms of living organisms. Emphasis is placed on novel collaborations that bring together scientists, preferably from different disciplines (e.g. chemistry, physics, computer science, engineering) to focus on problems in the life sciences http://www.hfsp.org/funding/eligible-countries

The Santa Fe Institute
The Santa Fe Institute is a private, not-for-profit, independent research and education center, founded in 1984, where leading scientists grapple with some of the most compelling and complex problems of our time. Researchers come to the Santa Fe Institute from universities, government agencies, research institutes, and private industry to collaborate across disciplines, merging ideas and principles of many fields – from physics, mathematics, and biology, to the social sciences and the humanities. http://www.santafe.edu/

International Society of Political Psychology (ISPP)
The ISPP is an interdisciplinary organization representing all fields of inquiry concerned with exploring the relationships between political and psychological processes. Members include psychologists, political scientists, psychiatrists, historians, sociologists, economists, and anthropologists, as well as journalists, government officials, and others. http://www.ispp.org/

Society for the Advancement of Socio-Economics (SASE)
The SASE is an international, interdisciplinary academic organization. The academic disciplines represented in the SASE include economics, sociology, political science, organization studies, management, psychology, law, and history https://sase.org/

The Resilience Alliance (RA)
The RA is a research organization comprised of scientists and practitioners from many disciplines who collaborate to explore the dynamics of social–ecological systems. The body of knowledge developed by the RA encompasses key concepts of resilience, adaptability, and transformability, and provides a foundation for sustainable development policy and practice. http://www.resalliance.org/

Integration and Implementation Sciences
Focusing on complex real-world problems, Integration and Implementation Sciences is a new discipline that aims to prepare and support scientists to engage in such transdisciplinary projects and work towards policy and practice change. The website aims to be a hub for these 'I2S'. http://i2s.anu.edu.au/

International Center for Transdisciplinary Research (CIRET)
The International Center for Transdisciplinary Research was founded in Paris in 1987 and is a network for scientists, educators and others who aim to connect sciences, culture and ethics, acknowledging the complexity of reality. More than most kindred organizations, this network has a relatively strong presence outside the Anglophone world. http://ciret-transdisciplinarity.org

Science of Team Science
As science projects are increasingly conducted by collaborative teams of scientists, it has become more relevant for scientists, funding agencies and policymakers to have more insights in assembling, coordinating and evaluating such team science. Hence, the development of the science of team science in 2008. The SciTS website provides resources and toolkits for both conducting and studying team science. http://www.scienceofteamscience.org/

References

Abma, R. (2011). *Over de Grenzen van Disciplines – Plaatsbepaling van de Sociale Wetenschappen*. Nijmegen: Uitgeverij Vantilt.

Barkley, R. (2006). *Attention Deficit Hyperactivity Disorder: A Handbook for Diagnosis and Treatment* (3rd ed.). New York: The Guilford Press.

Berkes, F. (2003). Alternatives to conventional management: Lessons from small-scale fisheries. *Environments, 31*, 5–19.

Caetano, R., Schafer, J. & Cunradi, C.B. (2001). Alcohol-related intimate partner violence among white, black, and Hispanic couples in the United States. *Alcohol Research & Health, 25*, 58–65.

Chalmers, A.F. (1999). *What is this Thing called Science?* Maidenhead: Open University Press.

Charles, A.T. (1994). Towards sustainability: the fishery experience. *Ecological Economics, 11*, 201–211.

Cooper, J. M. (ed.) (1997). *Plato; Complete Works*. Cambridge: Hackett Publishing Company.

Eigenbrode, S.D., O'Rourke, M., Wulfhorst, J.D., Althoff, D.M., Goldberg, C.S., et al. (2007). Employing philosophical dialogue in collaborative science. *BioScience, 57*, 55–64.

Fish, E.W, Faccidomo, S. & Miczek, K.A. (1999). Aggression heightened by alcohol or social instigation in mice: reduction by the 5-HT B receptor agonist CP-94,253. *Psychopharmacology, 146*, 391–399.

Frodeman, R., Klein, J.T. & Mitcham, C. (eds.) (2010). *The Oxford Handbook of Interdisciplinarity*. Oxford: Oxford University Press.

Garcia, S.M. & Cochrane, K.L. (2005). Ecosystem approach to fisheries: A review of implementation guidelines. *ICES Journal of Marine Science, 62*, 311–318.

Hirsch-Hadorn, G., Hoffmann-Riem, H., Biber-Klemm S., Grossenbacher-Mansuy, W., Joye, D., et al. (eds.) (2008). *Handbook of transdisciplinary research*. Dordrecht: Springer.

Holland, J.H. (2006). Studying complex adaptive systems. *Journal of Systems Science and Complexity, 19*, 1-8.

Le Treut, H., Somerville, R., Cubasch, U., Ding, Y., Mauritzen, C., et al. (2007). Historical overview of climate change. In: S. Solomon, D. Qin, M. Manning, Z. Chen, M. Marquis, et al. (eds.), *Climate Change 2007: The Physical Science Basis. Contribution of Working Group I to the Fourth Assessment Report of the Intergovernmental Panel on Climate Change* (p. 93-127). Cambridge: Cambridge University Press.

Jury, W.A. & Vaux, H. Jr. (2005). The role of science in solving the world's emerging water problems. *Proceedings of the National Academy of Sciences of the USA, 44*, 15715-15720.

Keestra, M. (2012). Understanding Human Action – Integrating Meanings, Mechanisms, Causes, and Contexts. In: A.F. Repko, W.H. Newell & R. Szostak (eds.), *Case Studies in Interdisciplinary Research* (p. 225-258). Thousand Oaks, CA: Page Publications.

Klein, J.T. & Newell, W. (1997). Advancing interdisciplinary studies. In: J. G. Gaff & J. Ratcliff (eds.), *Handbook of the Undergraduate Curriculum* (p. 393-394). San Francisco: Jossey-Bass.

Klein, J.T. (1990). *Interdisciplinarity – History, Theory and Practice*. Detroit: Wayne State University Press.

Krishnan, A. (2009). *What are Academic Disciplines? Some Observations on the Disciplinarity vs. Interdisciplinarity Debate* (ESRC national centre for research methods working paper series 03/09). Southampton: University of Southampton.

Lélé, S. & Norgaard, R.B. (2005). Practicing interdisciplinarity. *BioScience, 55*, 967-975.

Levin, S.A. (1998). Ecosystems and the biosphere as complex adaptive systems. *Ecosystems, 1*, 431-436.

Mann, M.E., Bradley, R.S. & Hughes, M.K. (1999). Northern hemisphere temperatures during the past millennium: inferences, uncertainties, and limitations. *Geophysical Research Letters, 26*, 759-762.

Mitchell, M. (2009). *Complexity – A Guided Tour*. New York: Oxford University Press.
National Academy of Sciences (2005). *Facilitating Interdisciplinary Research*.
Washington: The National Academies Press.

National Science Foundation (2001). *NSF GPRA Strategic Plan FY 2001-2005*.
Arlington, VA: National Science Foundation.

Newell, W.H. (2006). Interdisciplinary integration by undergraduates. *Issues in Integrative Studies, 24*, 89-111.

Newell, W.H. (2007). Chapter 13 "Decision making in interdisciplinary studies". In:
Göktug Morçöl (ed.) *Handbook of Decision Making in Interdisciplinary Studies* (p. 245-264). New York: CRC Press/Taylor & Francis Group.

Page, S.E. (2010). *Diversity and Complexity*. Princeton, NJ: Princeton University Press.

Paul, R. & Elder, L. (2014). *The Miniature Guide to Critical Thinking Concepts and Tools*. Tomales, CA: The Foundation for Critical Thinking.

Popper, K.R. (1963). *Conjectures and Refutations: The Growth of Scientific Knowledge*. London: Routledge.

Repko, A.F. (2007). Integrating interdisciplinarity: How the theories of common ground and cognitive interdisciplinarity are forming the debate on interdisciplinary integration. *Issues in Integrative Studies, 25*, 1-31.

Repko, A.F. (2012). *Interdisciplinary Research – Process and Theory (2nd edition)*.
Thousand Oaks, CA: Sage Publications.

Rittel, H.W.J. & Webber, M.M. (1973). Dilemmas in a general theory of planning.
Policy Sciences, 4, 155-169.

Salisbury, F. & Ross, C. (1985). *Plant Physiology*. Belmont, CA: Wadsworth Publishing Company.

van Santen, R.A., Khoe, D. & Vermeer, B. (2010). *2030 – Technology that will Change the World*. New York: Oxford University Press.

Scheffer, M., Carpenter, S., Foley, J.A., Folke, C. & Walker, B. (2001). Catastrophic shifts in ecosystems. *Nature, 4*, 591-596.

Talisayon, S.D. (2010, March 28). Group Mind Mapping. *Apin Talisayon's weblog*.
Consulted on https://apintalisayon.wordpress.com/

Valli, K. (2011). Dreaming in the multilevel framework. *Consciousness and Cognition, 20*, 1084-1090.

World Commission on Environment and Development (1987). *Our Common Future*. Oxford: Oxford University Press.

References
Research projects undertaken by IIS students

Aarts, I., van Dijk, N. & Voermans, E. (2012). Bachelor thesis: *Het Nut van Zelfmoordterrorisme.*

Bakker, T., van der Linden, I., Steenbrink, M., Stuut, M. & Veldhuyzen van Zanten, S. (2014). Bachelor thesis: *Fogponics: Richting een Duurzaam Alternatief voor Landbouw.*

Beukenhorst, A., Huygen, M. & van Leeuwen, R. (2012). Bachelor thesis: *Elektriciteitsvoorziening van de Toekomst; Smart Grids op een Studentenwooncampus.*

Bekius, F. & Elsenburg, L. (2010). Bachelor thesis: *De Invloed van Omega-3 Vetzuren en Meetmethode op HRV bij Mannen en Vrouwen.*

Cederhout, M., Dodu, A. & Perrin, K. (2012). Bachelor thesis: *Door Diëten Minder Druk?*

van Dierendonck, R.C.H., van Egmond, M.A.N.E., ten Hagen, D.L. & Kreuning, J. (2013). Bachelor thesis: *De Dodo op de Weegschaal. Een Verscherping van de Regressiemethode ter Bepaling van het Gewicht van Raphus cucullatus.*

Dijkgraaf, F., Hooghiemstra, M. & van der Spoel, I. (2009). Bachelor thesis: *Samenwerking tussen Tumorcellen, Beslissing Maken en Speltheorie. Waarom Werken Tumorcellen Samen?*

van Dun, L., Muller, R. & Boeke, N. (2012). Bachelor thesis: *Welke Locaties in Mexico zijn Vanuit Duurzaam Perspectief Geschikt voor het Produceren van Zeegolfenergie en in Welk Percentage van de Huidige Energieconsumptie kan Worden Voorzien?*

Elands, J. (2011). Bachelor thesis: *Je Buurt, Je Baan: Een Onderzoek naar Gevoelens van Uitsluiting op de Arbeidsmarkt.*

Gelauff, M.N.A., Gravemaker, W.L., Isarin, A.L. & Waajen, A.C. (2015). Bachelor thesis: *Natriumsulfaatmist: Effect op lichtintensiteit, bodemsamenstelling en de groei van gewassen.*

Kam, L., Nieuwland, M. & Tan, J. (2011). Bachelor thesis: *Het Placebo-effect van Lichttherapie.*

Maan, M.C.L., Cupido, A.J. & Moll, M.W. (2012). Bachelor thesis: *De Rationalizer: Bewustzijn over Emoties als Handvat voor Rationele Beslissingen.*

Noyon, L. (2012). Bachelor thesis: *"Maar dat zijn Sentimenten!" Een Onderzoek naar de Ongemakkelijke Relatie tussen Rechtspraak en een Gepolitiseerde Veiligheidsobsessie.*

Olthof, M., Bulters, T. & Zwennes, O. (2011). Bachelor thesis: *Een Analyse van de Toepassing van Real-time Stress Diagnosesystemen voor het Dagelijks Leven.*

Post, P., van der Roest, E. &. Witteveen, F. (2012). Bachelor thesis: *Patroonvorming op de Schelp van L. castrensis.*

Schram, R. (2012). Bachelor thesis: *Vrijwilligerstoerisme, een Vloek of een Zegen?*

Sier, R., Dreef, C., Jansen, A. & Ter Beek, R. (2011). Bachelor thesis: *Symmetrische Schoonheid: een Evolutionair Mechanisme dat Open Staat voor Socio-culturele Invloeden.*

van Wijchen, D., Hibender, J. & Amersfoort, R. (2012). Bachelor thesis: *Hoe Beïnvloedt het Empathisch Vermogen Menselijke Inter-temporele Beslissingen met Betrekking tot Geld?*

Colophon

University of Amsterdam

The University of Amsterdam (UvA), with some 30,000 students, 5,000 staff, and a budget of more than 600 million euros, is one of the largest comprehensive universities in Europe. Teaching and research at the UvA are conducted at seven faculties: the Humanities, Social and Behavioural Sciences, Economics and Business, Law, Science, and Medicine and Dentistry, with programs offered in almost every field.

The Institute for Interdisciplinary Studies

The Institute for Interdisciplinary Studies (IIS) is a knowledge center for interdisciplinary learning and teaching. Each year, the institute provides a diversity of interdisciplinary education to some 3,300 students enrolled in bachelor's or master's programs or open courses. In recent years, dozens of lecturers in different disciplines from within and outside the UvA have contributed to education or other activities in the institute. The Institute is a 'laboratory' for interdisciplinary experiments and projects that might lead to new interdisciplinary courses, teaching methods, or programs. The IIS conducts assignments and projects for clients both within and outside the UvA. It also advises on interdisciplinary education.

Editors

- Prof. dr. Steph B.J. Menken: Professor of Evolutionary Biology at the Institute for Biodiversity and Ecosystem Dynamics and Scientific Director of the IIS, Faculty of Science, UvA.
- Dr. M. Keestra: Assistant professor of philosophy at the IIS Faculty of Science, UvA and President of the international Association for Interdisciplinary Studies.

Authors

- L. Rutting MSc: Lucas is a lecturer at the IIS. He specializes in ecology and socio-ecological systems.
- G. Post MSc: Ger is a lecturer at the IIS. His specialty is brain and cognitive sciences.
- M. de Roo MSc: Mieke is a lecturer at the IIS. Her specialty is human and political geography.
- S. Blad MSc: Sylvia is a former lecturer at the IIS. She specializes in the philosophy of biology.
- L. de Greef MSc: Linda is a programme manager at Het Onderwijslab, IIS. She specializes in interdisciplinary teaching and learning.

Contact

Institute for Interdisciplinary Studies
Science Park 904
1098 XH Amsterdam
Tel. +31 20 525 51 90
www.iis.uva.nl
Onderwijslab-iis@uva.nl